HTML5 Game Programming with enchant.js

Brandon McInnis

Ryo Shimizu

Hidekazu Furukawa

Ryohei Fushimi

Ryo Tanaka

Kevin Kratzer

Apress·

HTML5 Game Programming with enchant.js

ISBN-13 (pbk): 978-1-4302-4743-2

ISBN-13 (electronic): 978-1-4302-4774-9

President and Publisher: Paul Manning
Lead Editor: Ben Renow-Clarke
Developmental Editor: Barbara McGuire
Technical Reviewer: Foaad Khosmood
Editorial Board: Steve Anglin, Mark Beckner, Ewan Buckingham, Gary Cornell, Louise Corrigan, Morgan Ertel,
    Jonathan Gennick, Jonathan Hassell, Robert Hutchinson, Michelle Lowman, James Markham,
    Matthew Moodie, Jeff Olson, Jeffrey Pepper, Douglas Pundick, Ben Renow-Clarke, Dominic Shakeshaft,
    Gwenan Spearing, Matt Wade, Tom Welsh
Coordinating Editor: Anamika Panchoo
Copy Editor: Lori Cavanaugh
Compositor: SPi Global
Indexer: SPi Global
Artist: SPi Global
Cover Designer: Anna Ishchenko

Distributed to the book trade worldwide by Springer Science+Business Media New York, 233 Spring Street, 6th Floor, New York, NY 10013. Phone 1-800-SPRINGER, fax (201) 348-4505, e-mail orders-ny@springer-sbm.com, or visit www.springeronline.com. Apress Media, LLC is a California LLC and the sole member (owner) is Springer Science + Business Media Finance Inc (SSBM Finance Inc). SSBM Finance Inc is a Delaware corporation.

For information on translations, please e-mail rights@apress.com, or visit www.apress.com.

Apress and friends of ED books may be purchased in bulk for academic, corporate, or promotional use. eBook versions and licenses are also available for most titles. For more information, reference our Special Bulk Sales–eBook Licensing web page at www.apress.com/bulk-sales.

Any source code or other supplementary materials referenced by the author in this text is available to readers at www.apress.com. For detailed information about how to locate your book's source code, go to www.apress.com/source-code.

For Derek, Dad, and Patti.
"Just keep swimming."
—Finding Nemo

Contents at a Glance

Contents

About the Authors

Brandon McInnis is the Technical Evangelist for enchant.js at the Akihabara Research Center at Ubiquitous Entertainment, Inc. in Tokyo and has a background in web development. He has an unlikely past that involves singing opera and interpreting for the original composer of the Final Fantasy video game series, Nobuo Uematsu. When he's not developing for the web or educating users on enchant.js, he enjoys spending time writing and recording music and adventuring around Tokyo.

Ryo Shimizu dropped out of the University of Electronic Communication and was recognized by the government of Japan as a Genius Programmer/Super-creator in 2005. He lectured at Kyushu University from 2008 to 2010, and has been the President and CEO of Ubiquitous Entertainment, Inc. since 2003. He lives in Akihabara, and his hobbies include wine tasting.

Hidekazu Furukawa is a Technical Writer at Ubiquitous Entertainment, Inc., and has authored several successful books in Japan on mobile development and gaming.

Ryohei Fushimi currently studies at the University of Tokyo in the engineering department. He is the enchant.js dev team leader at Ubiquitous Entertainment, Inc. and, though originally from Okayama, currently lives in Tokyo.

Ryo Tanaka is a student in the Department of Information Science at the University of Tokyo's School of Science. She developed the core of enchant.js.

Kevin Kratzer grew up in Germany and is currently studying for his Master of Science in Informatics degree at Technical University of Munich. He has worked on several software projects as both a developer and software architect, including enchant.js. He currently lives in Munich and works for Ubiquitous Entertainment, Inc. developing for mobile and web.

About the Technical Reviewer

Foaad Khosmood is Forbes Professor of Computer Engineering at California Polytechnic State University, where he teaches Interactive Entertainment Engineering and other courses. He holds a Ph.D. in Computer Science from the University of California, Santa Cruz. Foaad is an officer of the non-profit Global Game Jam Inc., and has served as its chief technologist since Global Game Jam 2009.

Foaad's research interests include AI, natural language processing, machine learning, and interactive entertainment and systems.

Acknowledgments

I would first like to thank Anamika Panchoo, the most patient Coordinating Editor in the world, for her expert guidance and support during the authoring of this book. Without her guiding hand, this never would have come to fruition. She was motivating and uplifting in her e-mails, especially on the many nights I stayed up until odd hours of the morning to meet chapter deadlines. Ana, your encouragement made this whole process much more palatable. Thank you.

Also, I would like to thank Barbara McGuire for her massive contributions to how the book could be improved in terms of organization and approach. Her extensive knowledge of the technical writing world proved invaluable to how I wrote (and rewrote) most of the manuscript, and is the sole reason for how the book is organized around incremental step-by-step instruction. Barbara, this entire book is much easier to digest because of you.

A big thank you as well to Dr. Foaad Khosmood at California Polytechnic State University for very constructive suggestions and guidance on some of the chapters. Your familiarity with academia and the textbook world was valuable and effective in helping me develop many sections in the manuscript to be more succinct, relevant, and correct.

Although uncredited in the author list, Eric McEver did a substantial amount of translation from the original Japanese version of this book. Although I am very grateful to him for greatly reducing the amount of translation I was required to do to compile source material for this publication, it is only by virtue of his introduction to Ubiquitous Entertainment, Inc. that I am now living and working in Tokyo. Words cannot express my gratitude, Eric. There's no doubt you changed my life. To everyone reading, Eric is currently studying film directing at the graduate level in Singapore, and I sincerely believe we will be seeing his masterpieces, which offer refreshing and new windows into Japanese culture, on the big screen someday. Check out his films at ericmcever.com!

To everyone back home in the USA, thank you so much for your support. Moving to the other side of the world has been and continues to be an amazing experience, but comes with its own special blend of trying times. Derek, Dad, Mama Patti, Kati, Michael, Maddie, and Jonathan: I am grateful to each and every one of you for your messages and Skype calls. Truly, they have gotten me through difficult times while writing this book here in the New York of Asia. And Jonathan, thanks for the headshot! Your booming photography business (mcinnisphotography.com) and talent for portraits never cease to amaze me.

—Brandon McInnis

Introduction

If you're reading this, you undoubtedly have some level of interest in making games for the web. As someone with some experience in this field, I feel qualified to tell you you're in the right place.

Games on the web have changed immensely in the last ten years and, while the core concepts of web games tend to change very slowly over time, the tools we use to create them change much more rapidly. On today's web, large amounts of code must be written to accomplish simple, game-related tasks in a browser.

The open-source game engine enchant.js solves this problem by drastically reducing the amount of code needed to write a game, and includes several fall-back and compatibility functions that work behind the scenes to keep things running smoothly across multiple browsers without you needing to do anything special. It has become a very popular tool in its home country in Japan, and is now being used more and more by programmers in the West.

If you're a beginner to web coding, don't worry! We walk you step-by-step through the basics of how enchant.js works, JavaScript (the common scripting language of the web – used by enchant.js), and basic elements of an enchant.js game. We then move on to more advanced topics. We cover all the necessities of a game, including scenes, sprites, interactivity, and more. Additionally, we provide tutorials for every concept. In the second part of the book, we show you how to create several games, including a Whack-A-Mole game (in 2-D and 3-D) and a classic arcade space shooter.

Although some code samples in the book are linked to working versions on the free programming environment code.9leap.net, all code samples in this book can be found at the Apress website (www.apress.com) by searching for this title and going to the source code section of this book's page.

Learning game programming is a fun and exciting adventure with entertaining rewards. If you have a question regarding the library, please don't hesitate to reach out to us on the official enchant.js subreddit (reddit.com/r/enchantjs), enchantjs.com, or our Facebook page (search for "enchant.js"). Our user community is growing every day with both brand new and experienced game programmers.

Best of luck on your game programming journey!
Brandon McInnis
enchant.js Technical Evangelist

CHAPTER 1

■ ■ ■

Beginning enchant.js Development

The enchant.js framework was developed at the Ubiquitous Entertainment Inc. (UEI) Akihabara Research Center in Tokyo and was originally released in April, 2011. It has enjoyed considerable popularity in Japan ever since and has a growing base of fans from other countries. The enchant.js framework is an HTML5 and JavaScript-based game engine and stand-alone code library that enables you to develop applications that can run on a PC or Mac or on iPhone, iPad, and Android devices. Although game applications created using the engine can be run on many different kinds of devices, most have been created and optimized for smartphone use.

The decline of Adobe Flash as an interactive platform in recent years has led modern web game developers to turn to other browser-based and ubiquitous platforms, such as HTML5 and JavaScript, to create browser-based experiences for their users. However, while JavaScript originally was developed to be a language accessible to non-professional developers, the complexity of JavaScript used today for game authoring in the browser often requires a large investment of time to learn and use efficiently. As an open-source game library, enchant.js reduces this complexity by providing game authoring functionality for developers, which significantly minimizes your learning curve for writing browser-based games and increases the speed of your game development.

With this book, you can start creating and publishing games quickly and easily. Don't worry if you're a complete beginner to programming. We take you through all the basics so you can get up and running fast. If you are at an intermediate level, we provide advanced content for you as well. We describe the different parts of the enchant.js framework and create several games, including classic games like Whack-A-Mole and arcade shooters, along the way to acquaint you with all the enchant.js library has to offer.

Visit the enchant.js Web Sites

To get a quick start with enchant.js, take a look at the three main enchant.js web sites. Each site has specific functions that help you create and share games faster and easier.

- `http://enchantjs.com`: download the enchant.js code library, find resources, and read programming tips
- `http://code.9leap.net`: develop, edit, and test games in an online, cloud-based environment
- `http://9leap.net`: upload, play, and share games

The main enchant.js site is where you can learn about the library and download the source code to develop your own games. You can also develop games in an online environment on `code.9leap.net` for a streamlined experience. After developing your game, you can post it to `9leap.net`. Figure 1-1 shows the basic relationship of the sites.

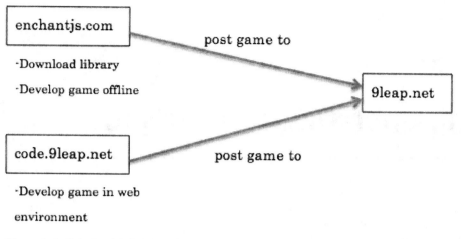

Figure 1-1. *Relationship between the web sites*

enchantjs.com

The official enchant.js web site at http://enchantjs.com provides reference information about the library, tutorials, tips, and resources. The site is updated regularly with posts from enchant.js developers regarding new versions and features and is fully bilingual in Japanese and English. The site's default language is English. If the Japanese version happens to appear and you want the English version to be displayed, use the flag icon on the right side of the screen to change the language back to English. Figure 1-2 shows the home page of enchant.js.

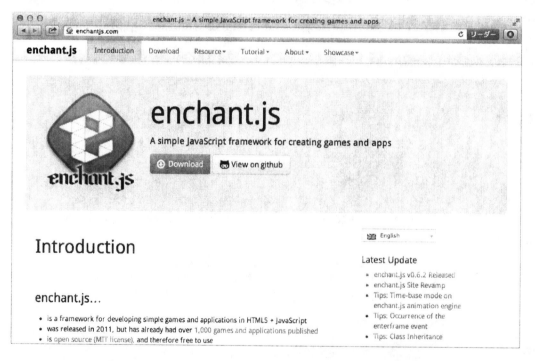

Figure 1-2. *enchantjs.com home page*

code.9leap.net

On the `http://code.9leap.net` web site, you can perform HTML/JavaScript editing, testing, and sharing directly within a web browser. The `code.9leap.net` site supports the import of enchant.js as well as easy uploading to `9leap.net`, allowing the entire game development cycle, from programming to publication, to take place in the browser. It can be used on a PC or Mac or on devices such as an iPad.

Figure 1-3 shows the `code.9leap.net` log-in page. At the time of publication of this book, the site is in a beta stage of development.

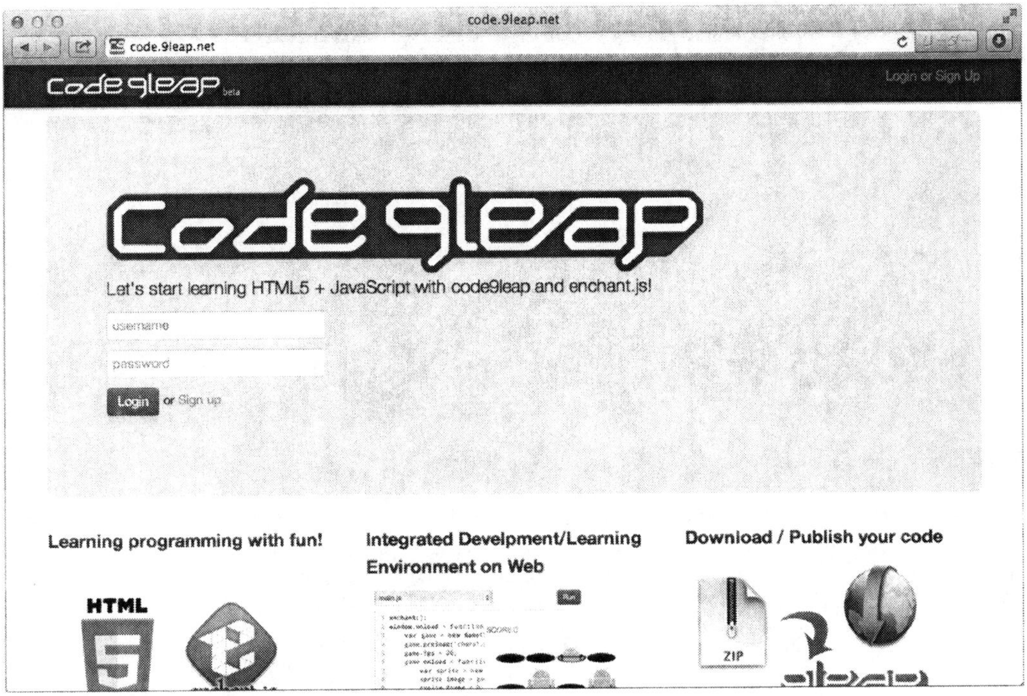

Figure 1-3. `code.9leap.net` log-in page

9leap.net

The 9leap site at `http://global.9leap.net` is hosted by UEI and D2 Communications (`www.d2c.co.jp/en`) and was launched with the aim of discovering and promoting young developers. The site allows you to upload, play, and share games. The 9leap site includes numerous games that developers like you have created with enchant.js. Try out some of the games on the site to get a feel for enchant.js before you start to create your own games. Figure 1-4 shows the 9leap home page.

Figure 1-4. 9leap.net home page

You can also enter game development contests on the site. Contest finalists win prizes such as the latest PC and Mac computers, bookstore gift cards, and more. Additionally, as part of the 9leap project UEI regularly hosts 9leap game programming camps in Japan and is beginning to host camps in the United States as well. Typically, these camps begin with a seminar on game programming and provide guidance to help participants create a simple game of their own. For more information, see the enchantjs.com web site.

Compatibility and Releases

The following browsers and devices support enchant.js:

- Internet Explorer (IE) 9.0 and later
- Chrome 10 and later for Mac OS X, Windows, and Linux
- Safari 5 and later for Mac OS X and Windows
- Firefox 3.6 and later for Mac OS X and Windows
- iOS 4 and later for the iPhone and iPad
- Android 2.1 and later

Table 1-1 shows the major releases of enchant.js. At the time of the publication of this book, the latest version of enchant.js is version 0.6.2.

Table 1-1. *Recent Releases and Added Functionality of enchant.js*

Version	Functions Added
0.6.2 (current)	• Better performance on Android • Improved keybinding
0.6.1	• Improved WebAudio • Improved timeline
0.6.0	• WebAudio API • DOM/Canvas rendering • Animation engine • Core class
0.5.2	• Time-based animation (tl.enchant.js)
0.5.1	• Bug-fixes
0.5.0	• Sound support on iPhone • Support for rotation & scale properties • Canvas support • ElapsedTime support

■ **Note** As of version 0.6.1, enchant.js is licensed under the MIT license. Contact Ubiquitous Entertainment (http://global.uei.co.jp/) with inquiries about corporate use of code created with enchant.js.

Features of enchant.js

Designed to make game programming simpler, enchant.js comes with several features to make it easier for developers, whether expert or novice, to create games. The main features of the library are its object-oriented methodology, the specific way it processes game code, its extensibility through plug-ins, and its content library.

Object-Oriented Programming

Object-oriented programming (OOP) is a methodology that emphasizes the objects being operated on rather than the process of operation. To illustrate this concept, each graphic that can be displayed on the screen in enchant.js is an object. What is actually visible on the screen is part of another object, called the display object tree. By issuing a command to join a graphic object to the display object tree, the graphic object becomes visible onscreen.

Listing 1-1 shows a player object and an enemy character object being created and displayed on the screen by registration in the display object tree. For now, don't worry about the specifics of how this code works. We provide a code sample here simply to give you a quick look at OOP in action. We walk you through code samples in detail later.

Listing 1-1. Using Object-Oriented Programming to Create Two Objects and Add Them Onscreen

```
//Player object creation
var player = new Sprite(32, 32);
player.image = game.assets['player.png'];
```

```
//Enemy character object creation
var enemy = new Sprite(32, 32);
enemy.image = game.assets['enemy.png'];

//Registration in the display object tree
var scene = game.currentScene;
scene.addChild(player);
scene.addChild(enemy);
```

Asynchronous Processing

Asynchronous processing is processing that is run independent of a main set of code. Think of this as multitasking. If a computer is receiving lines of commands to be run one after the other, and then begins receiving commands to run other commands while the first set is still being run, this is an example of asynchronous processing.

Operations or events initiated by the user or other programs are processed by enchant.js asynchronously. When the user does not issue any commands, the program simply waits without doing anything instead of running code continuously in the background. In addition, when the user is forced to wait for a program to complete processing, this asynchronous nature makes it possible to issue other commands at the same time.

Listing 1-2 shows sections of code designated to be run when specific events occur. This is called *event handling*. In this code sample, we handle the player object in each frame and we also handle touch events. Specifically, every time a frame is drawn, we want some code to run (or "be executed" as developers sometimes say). When a user playing the game clicks or "touches" the character, we want different code to be executed. We cover this process in detail in Chapter 3.

Listing 1-2. Asynchronous Processing for the Creation, Setup, and Handling of a Character

```
//player (character) object creation
var player = new Sprite(32, 32);

//handling of the character in each frame
player.addEventListener(Event.ENTER_FRAME, function() {
    ...
});

//handling touch events
player.addEventListener(Event.TOUCH_START, function(e) {
    var x = e.localX;
    var y = e.localY;
    ...
});
```

Plug-in Extensibility

You can extend the features of enchant.js through various plug-ins to add more functionality. For example, some plug-ins allow you to develop games that support devices like D-pads and analog sticks or create interactive games that look like comic books. We show you how to use several of the plug-ins in later chapters of the book.

We don't provide an exhaustive list of all the enchant.js plug-ins here because you can find the list, along with detailed information about each plug-in, on the enchantjs.com web site. You can download the plug-ins (see the enchant.js download package) from the site.

Images and Sounds

If you are an independent game programmer, it can be challenging to find images to use for characters, monsters, scenery, and so on. Since enchant.js comes with a royalty-free (for non-commercial games) assortment of original game images, as well as material from previous UEI game releases, you can be spared the effort of creating images for your own games by using the image library. Images are included in the main enchant.js package. Figure 1-5 shows a few examples of the wide range of available character images.

Figure 1-5. *Examples of character images in the enchant.js package*

You can also download sounds in a zip file, separate from the main library, from the download page on enchantjs.com. For example, you can include background music, sounds of explosions, laser shots, gunshots, blips that could be used when a character picks up items, and more.

JavaScript, HTML5, and CSS

Modern web sites typically are built with a combination of three types of code: JavaScript, HTML5, and Cascading Style Sheets (CSS). Usually, HTML provides the core content, CSS is used to style and format it, and JavaScript is used to interact with page elements and provide animation. We provide brief summaries of HTML5 and CSS in this chapter, but this book overall largely focuses on JavaScript, as that is the language in which enchant.js games are written.

JavaScript

JavaScript is an object-oriented, interpreted programming language that was originally developed to add interactivity and movement to web pages. An example of JavaScript is shown in Listing 1-3. You might have heard of a programming language called Java, but it is completely different from JavaScript. JavaScript is guaranteed to work with all the major web browsers without any additional software installations. Do not worry if you have never seen JavaScript before! We'll cover it in detail in Chapter 2.

Listing 1-3. JavaScript Example That Displays "Hello, World!" on the Screen

```
document.write('<p>Hello, World!</p>');
```

HTML and HTML5

HTML is short for HyperText Markup Language, and is a markup language for describing text on the Web. In enchant. js, HTML is used to load in JavaScript and control certain browser operations on smartphones (such as scaling). An example is shown in Listing 1-4. If you open a normal text file, type the code from Listing 1-4 in it, and save it as "index.html," that file can be opened by your browser. The browser will display the words "Hello World! This is the content part of an HTML page."

Listing 1-4. HTML Example Showing Content in a Browser

```
<!DOCTYPE html>
<html>
    <head>
        <meta charset="utf-8">
        <meta name="viewport" content="width=device-width, user-scalable=no">
        <meta name="apple-mobile-web-app-capable" content="yes">
        <meta name="apple-mobile-web-app-status-bar-style" content="black-translucent">
        <title>HelloWorld</title>
        <style type="text/css">
            body {
                margin: 0;
            }
        </style>
    </head>
    <body>
<p>Hello World! This is the content part of an HTML page.</p>
    </body>
</html>
```

HTML5 is a general term for several new features of HTML. Table 1-2 shows examples of the main features.

Table 1-2. *New HTML5 Features*

New HTML feature	Description
<canvas> element	Supports drawing of 2-D graphics
<audio> element	Allows sound playback
<video> element	Supports video playback
Application cache	Allows execution of applications offline
Cross-domain messaging	Allows transfer of information between domains
XMLHttpRequest Level 2	
Web storage	Saves data using a client
SQL Database	
Indexed database	
Web workers	Supports background processing for improved user experience
Server-send events	Allows two-way communication with the server
Web sockets	
File API	Allows access to local files

In enchant.js, HTML5 functions are not directly used but are accessed through the enchant.js library. We do not provide a detailed discussion of HTML and HTML5 in this book.

CSS

CSS stands for Cascading Style Sheets and is used with HTML to define the appearance of a web page, such as color, text, and size. HTML can also be used for specifying the appearance of a page, but its proper use is to specify content and define the appearance of that content using CSS. Editing dynamic web pages is especially made easier using CSS. Listing 1-5 shows how to change the background of the body element of a web page to gray and specify the font.

Listing 1-5. Changing the Background of a Web Page and Specifying the Font

```
body { background-color: #DDDDDD; font: 30px sans-serif; }
```

In enchant.js, CSS functions are not used directly but are accessed through the enchant.js library. We do not provide a detailed discussion of CSS in this book.

Making "Hello World!" Appear on the Screen

For our first enchant.js application, we show you how to make a very simple program that creates a label that says "Hello World!" The purpose of this exercise is to show you in a simple way how the elements of an enchant.com game come together. We'll create games that are more complex later.

1. Go to enchantjs.com and click the Download button to download the latest enchant.js package (not the development version).

2. After unzipping the file, open a text editor, copy and paste the code shown in Listing 1-6, and save the file as "index.html" inside the folder the enchant.js package unzipped to.

    Listing 1-6. Index.html: Loading in enchant.js and the Main Game Code

    ```html
    <!DOCTYPE html>
    <html>
        <head>
            <meta charset="utf-8">
            <title>HelloWorld</title>
            <script type="text/javascript" src="enchant.js"></script>
            <script type="text/javascript" src="main.js"></script>
        </head>
        <body>
        </body>
    </html>
    ```

    The code specifies the file as an HTML file, tells the browser we are using UTF-8 character encoding (enchant.js is written in this encoding), gives it a title of "HelloWorld," and then tells it to load in our game code from a file called "main.js," which we'll create next.

3. Create a new file in your text editor, copy and paste the code shown in Listing 1-7, and save the file as "main.js" inside the same folder.

    Listing 1-7. Simple enchant.js Application Showing "Hello World!" Onscreen

    ```javascript
    enchant();
    var game;
    ```

```
window.onload = function(){
        game = new Core(320, 320);
        game.onload = function(){
                sign = new Label();
                sign.text = "Hello World!";
                game.rootScene.addChild(sign);
        };
        game.start();
};
```

The code in Listing 1-7 tells enchant.js to start up with the enchant(); command, create the game, and specify the dimensions of the game screen. After the page has completely loaded, we specify instructions that create a new label with the name of "sign," specify the text as "Hello World!", and then add it to the game screen. Finally, with game.start(), we run those instructions.

Now if you open up index.html in a browser, you should see the words "Hello World!" displayed on the screen. In this example, the only files being used are enchant.js, index.html, and main.js.

This is a very rudimentary example, but from it you can see that enchant.js gets loaded in by index.html, and index.html also loads in the game code we have written in main.js. Our next example will be more graphical in nature and introduces you to the online programming environment, code.9leap.net.

Create a Skating Bear

For our second enchant.js application, we make a bear skate from left to right across the screen, and we optimize the application for display on smartphones. You can find an example of the code we create at http://code.9leap.net/codes/show/19822.

As we mentioned earlier, code.9leap.net prepares all the necessary elements for coding games in enchant. js. We use code.9leap.net for this application, and we walk you through all the necessary steps. Please note that code.9leap.net is still in the beta stage and might have slight variations from the screenshots shown in this section.

The following steps show the overall development process for creating an enchant.js application on code.9leap.net. We cover each step in detail in the next sections.

1. Get started with your application

2. Import the enchant.js library

3. Edit the source code

4. Preview your results

5. Finish editing your source code

Get started with your application

The first step for developing a game on code.9leap.net is to create an account. The following steps show you how to create an account. If you have already created an account you can skip this step, log in, and move on to Project Creation.

We highly recommend using Google Chrome as your browser of choice when programming with enchant.js. Although good results have also been found using Safari and Firefox, we cannot vouch for the stability of Internet Explorer when interacting with either the enchant.js library or the web sites associated with enchant.js.

1. Open http://code.9leap.net in your favorite browser and click the Sign up link, which is located below the username and password input areas. See Figure 1-6. (If the Japanese site appears, scroll down and click Switch To English).

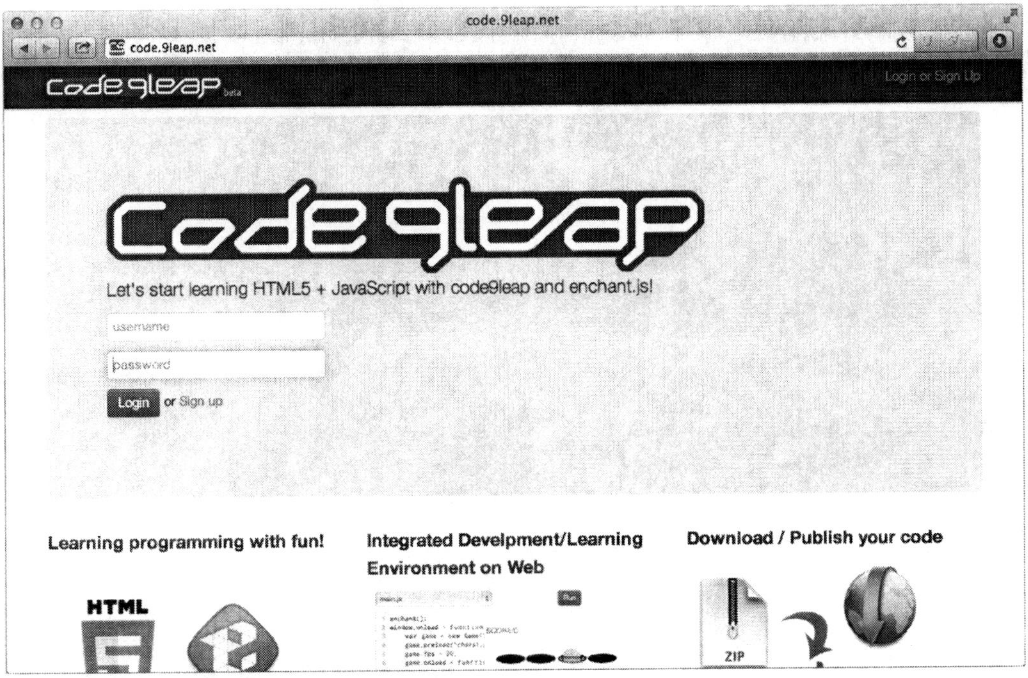

Figure 1-6. The `code.9leap.net` *login screen*

2. Choose a username and a password and enter them into their corresponding fields. Select "I agree to the Terms of Service" after you have read the terms of service. When you are finished, click the Sign up button located below the input form.

3. You will be redirected to the dashboard of your new account. An explanation of this screen follows in the next step. The next time you visit the site, you can just enter in your login information to log in.

After creating an account or logging in, you will be redirected to the dashboard, shown in Figure 1-7. The dashboard provides all necessary information regarding your account. On the right side you'll find a list of all projects you have created. (Of course, after creating a new account this list will initially be empty.) On the left side you'll find a Sample Projects list containing various categories.

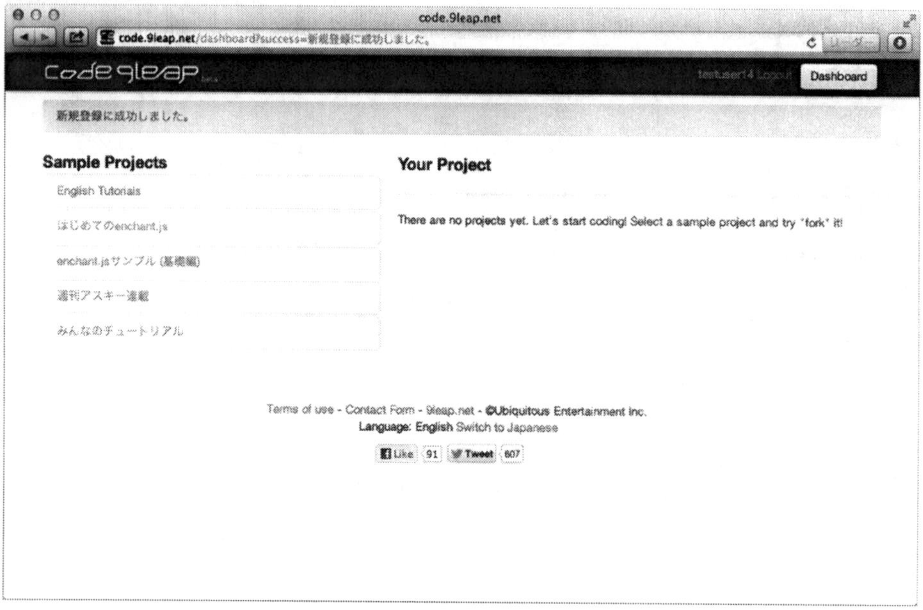

Figure 1-7. *The* `code.9leap.net` *dashboard*

To create an enchant.js application, you need to first create a project. A project is a package containing all the files necessary to manage an application. To develop one application, you need one project.

4. Click the English Tutorials category in the Sample Projects list, shown in Figure 1-8.

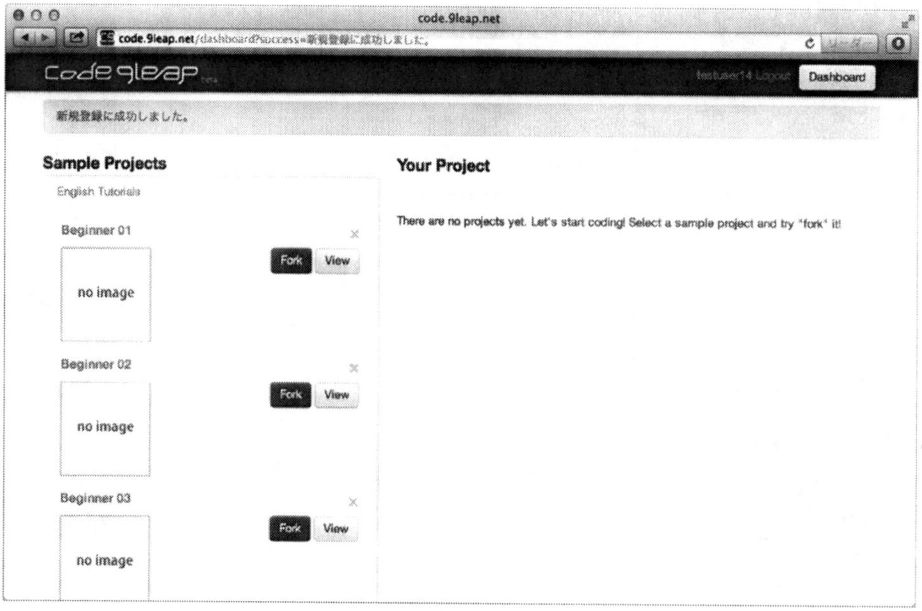

Figure 1-8. *English tutorials*

5. After you click a category, it will expand, displaying all projects in the category. You will see a list of Beginner projects that you can fork or view. Forking the project creates a copy in your project list. Viewing a project allows you to see the code together with a screen showing the result of the code when executed. Click Fork next to the Beginner 01 project. In the pop-up, confirm your action by clicking Fork again, as shown in Figure 1-9.

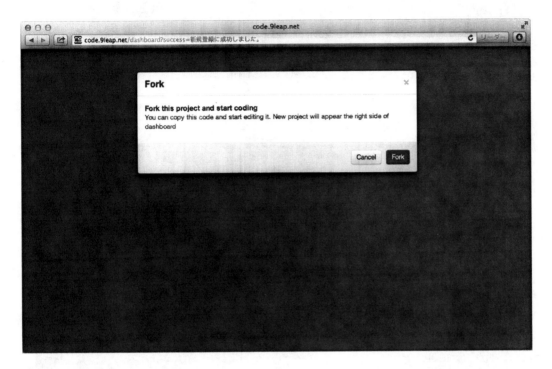

Figure 1-9. The Fork pop-up

6. After you click Fork for the second time, a source code editing screen is displayed with code already populated inside it. Shown in Listing 1-8, this code displays the string "Hello,Bear" using enchant.js, similar to the way we created the "Hello World!" program in a preceding section.

Listing 1-8. Show "Hello,Bear" on the Screen

```
enchant(); //the magic words that start enchant.js

window.onload = function() {
    game = new Game();
    game.onload = function() {              //Prepares the game
        hello = new Label("Hello,Bear");    //Create a new label with the words "Hello,Bear"
        hello.x = 10;                       //Place the label 10 pixels to the right
                                            //   (0 will always be the left border)
        hello.y = 150;                      //Place the label 150 pixels from the top
                                            //   (0 will always be the top border)

        game.rootScene.addChild(hello); //Show the label on the active screen
    }
    game.start(); //Begin the game
}
```

Just like in our earlier example, this code creates a label on the screen. Here, we place the label closer to the center of the screen and specify the text to be "Hello,Bear!" instead of "Hello World!" This time we won't use the source code, but will rewrite it to make our own enchant.js program. Figure 1-10 together with Table 1-3 show the different areas of the code editing screen.

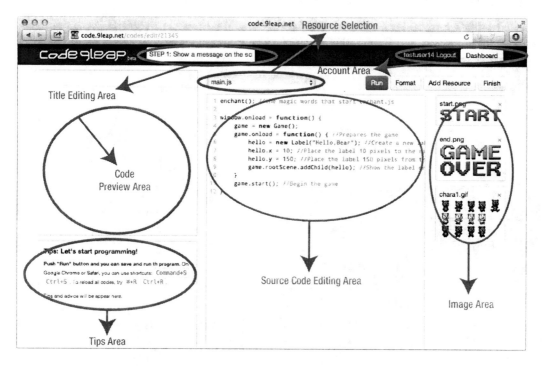

Figure 1-10. *Source code editing screen*

Table 1-3. *Elements of the Source Code Editing Screen*

Title Editing Area	The title of your application.
Account Area	Logout and dashboard access.
Code Preview Area	The code area that displays a preview of your application.
Tips Area	Tips or instructions for tutorials will be displayed here.
Resource Selection	A drop-down menu that enables you to switch between JavaScript (main.js), HTML (index.html), Cascading Style Sheets (style.css) and Tips (tips.json). By default, the menu is set to main.js. The drop-down menu is located directly above the code preview area.
Run Button	Executes the source code in the preview area.
Format Button	Formats the source code in the source code editing Area.
Add Resource Button	Used to add resources (images, sounds, and so on) used in the project.
Finish Button	Finishes source code editing and returns to the dashboard.
Source Code Editing Area	JavaScript source code, HTML file, and Tips editing. Also used when importing libraries.
Image Area	Displays all local images of the project.

Next, you need to edit the title (the application name).

7. Change the title in the title editing area (directly to the right of the code.9leap logo in the upper-right corner) on the source code editing screen. Enter "HelloEnchant" for now.

8. Change the title of the HTML file. Select index.html, which is the HTML file of the application, in the resource selection. The file will be displayed in the source code editing area, and should be prepopulated with some code. There you will find the title of the HTML file. In this case it is currently set to `<title>untitled</title>`. As shown in Figure 1-11, change it to `<title>HelloEnchant</title>` for our current application.

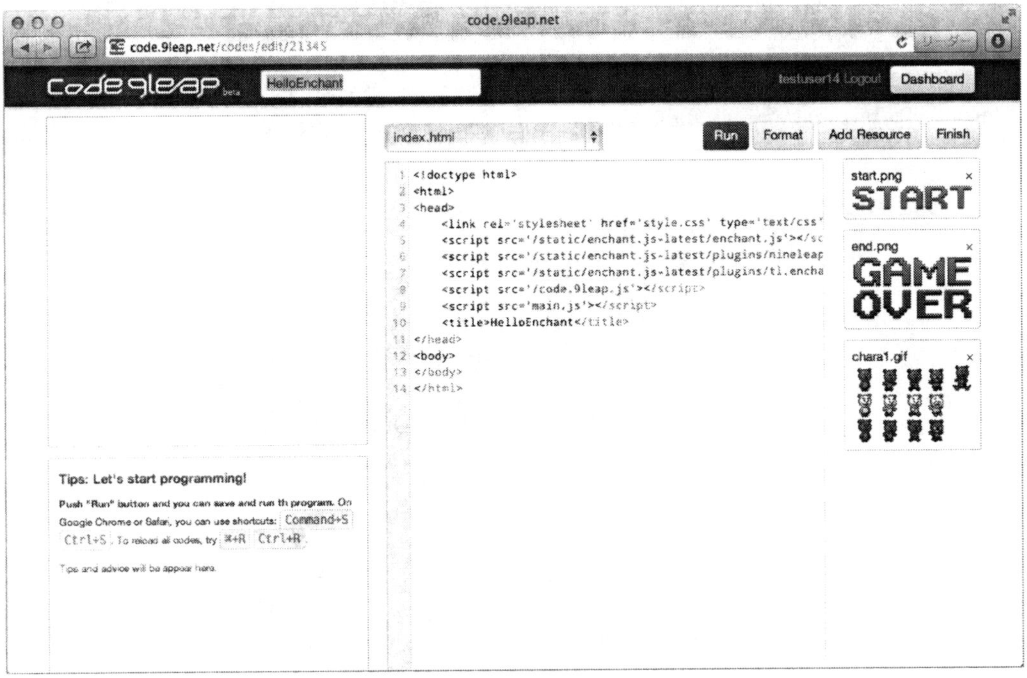

Figure 1-11. *Editing the title*

Import the enchant.js Library

A library is a file, or a group of files, that enables specific features to be used by other programs. To build our application, we use the enchant.js library. Libraries are loaded into a project by means of a script tag in an HTML file. Sometimes libraries require images to be added to a project, but we don't need to do that right now.

Keep in mind that plug-ins in enchant.js are also libraries, and thus they need their own script tag to be loaded. This is why you see lines referencing files such as `tl.enchant.js` and so on in the following listings.

To add the enchant.js library, do the following:

1. Remove the lines of code containing `nineleap.enchant.js` and `tl.enchant.js`. You should already be at index.html from the preceding steps. These lines of code will be inside the script tags (sections of code marked by `<script>`). These tags tell the browser that everything between `<script>` and `</script>` should be treated as a line of code. When `src=` is included in the script tag, it tells the browser to load lines of code from a file outside index.html. After removing the two lines of code, your `<script>` tags should match Listing 1-9.

Listing 1-9. Script Tags Loading enchant.js, Plug-ins, and Game Code

```
<script src='/static/enchant.js-latest/enchant.js'></script>
<script src='/code.9leap.js'></script>
<script src='main.js'></script>
```

▪ **Caution** The main.js script tag imports the application code, so this tag is always necessary. Never change or delete it.

You can use the code.9leap.js library to add any features that are required when you develop an enchant.js application in code.9leap.net; however, for our current application, don't make changes to the library. The /static/ enchant.js-latest/enchant.js tag imports the enchant.js library. When you develop applications in code.9leap.net, you can reference the newest release of enchant.js using the /static/enchant.js-latest/ path. The same goes for the enchant.js plug-ins nineleap.enchant.js and tl.enchant.js.

Edit the Source Code

To edit the source code, select main.js from the resource drop-down list. The screen should appear as it does in Figure 1-12.

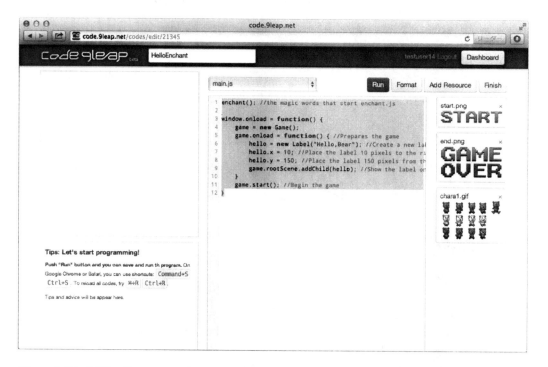

Figure 1-12. *Editing the source code*

Delete everything shown in the source code editing area because you need to copy and paste some code here. JavaScript distinguishes between upper and lower case, so be careful when copying code. Next, perform the following steps.

1. Initialize the enchant.js library. This allows you to use all the classes and methods included in the library. Listing 1-10 shows how to initialize the enchant.js library. The parentheses after the word "enchant" indicate that the previous word is a method, which runs a predefined set of code, and the semicolon at the end (;) indicates the end of a single statement of code.

   Listing 1-10. Initializing the enchant.js Library

   ```
   enchant();
   ```

2. On a new line under the enchant() method, designate code to be run after the page has loaded completely, as shown in Listing 1-11. Assigning code to the onload function of an object called the window, which, as you may suspect, represents the window in the browser, specifies that code to be run after loading.

   Listing 1-11. Designating Code to be Run After Loading Completes

   ```
   window.onload = function() {
       //code to be executed
   };
   ```

3. Create the core object by replacing "//code to be executed" with the code shown in Listing 1-12. The line that begins with two forward slashes indicates that the line is a comment, and will not be processed as code. To create a game, enchant.js needs a core object to add game elements to. Typing in "Core(320,320)" creates a game screen with a width of 320 pixels and a height of 320 pixels, respectively. The format of "new Core(320,320)" is called a constructor, and we use constructors to create new objects.

   Listing 1-12. Creating The Core Object

   ```
   var game = new Core(320, 320);
   ```

4. Preload the required image of a bear skating, as shown in Listing 1-13. To use images in enchant.js, you must preload them first. The image we load for this application is shown in Figure 1-13. Normally, this image must be uploaded into the code.9leap project or included in the same folder as your index.html file, but because we forked the project, this image is already in the project.

   Listing 1-13. Preloading The Image of a Bear Skating

   ```
   game.preload('chara1.gif');
   ```

Figure 1-13. The bear image: chara1.gif

5. Designate a function to be run once the game has loaded completely, as shown in Listing 1-14. We create this in much the same way as we did with `window.onload`, and we do this because any game object we create can be created successfully only if the core object has completely loaded.

Listing 1-14. Creating the game.onload Function

```
game.onload = function() {

};
```

6. Create the bear sprite, as shown in Listing 1-15. We must first create a new variable as a new `Sprite` object, with dimensions of 32 pixels wide by 32 pixels high, specify the image we preloaded to be used as the image of the bear, and then specify which part of the image we want to use. We want to use the image of the skating bear, which is the fifth image counting from the top left. Frame numbering begins with 0, so the skating bear is frame number 4 within the image. Note that this code must be typed inside the curly braces of the `game.onload` function.

Listing 1-15. Creating the Bear Sprite

```
var bear = new Sprite(32, 32);
bear.image = game.assets['chara1.gif'];
bear.frame=4;
```

7. Create an event listener to move the bear by three pixels to the right every frame, as shown in Listing 1-16. We cover event listeners in more detail later, but for now simply be aware that this code tells the program to move the bear every frame. Add it after the code you entered in Listing 1-16, still inside the `game.onload` curly braces.

Listing 1-16. Creating an Event Listener to Move the Bear

```
bear.addEventListener(Event.ENTER_FRAME, function() {
    this.x += 3; //move by 3 pixels
});
```

8. Add the bear to the game's root scene, as shown in Listing 1-17. We've created the bear, but it still won't be shown on the screen unless we add it to the game's root, or main, scene. Enter this code after the code you entered in Listing 1-16, still inside the `game.onload` curly braces.

Listing 1-17. Adding The Bear to the Game's Root Scene

```
game.rootScene.addChild(bear);
```

9. Under the game.onload curly braces, but still inside the `window.onload` curly braces, start the game. See Listing 1-18.

Listing 1-18. Starting the Game

```
game.start();
```

10. Check your code. Your code should match what is shown in Listing 1-19. You can ignore the comments (lines starting with two forward slashes). If it all matches, hit the Run button in the upper-right corner, and you should see your bear skate across the screen!

Listing 1-19. Making The Bear Skate Across the Screen

```
//initialization of enchant.js
enchant();

//code written here will be executed once the HTML file is completely loaded
window.onload = function() {
    //game object creation
    var game = new Core(320, 320);

    //image loading
    game.preload('chara1.gif');

    //execution once the image has loaded completely
    game.onload = function() {
        //Sprite creation
        var bear = new Sprite(32, 32);
        bear.image = game.assets['chara1.gif'];
        bear.frame=4;

        //frame loop to move the bear every frame
        bear.addEventListener(Event.ENTER_FRAME, function() {
            this.x += 3; //move by 3 pixels
        });

        //add the bear to the display object tree
        game.rootScene.addChild(bear);
    };
    game.start();
};
```

Now let's add some information to optimize the player experience on smartphones.

11. Select the index.html file from the resource drop-down menu. Adjust the content of your file to match the content shown in Listing 1-20.

Listing 1-20. Adjusting HTML for Smartphones

```
<!doctype html>
<html>
<head>
    <meta charset="utf-8">
    <meta name="viewport" content="width=device-width, user-scalable=no">
    <meta name="apple-mobile-web-app-capable" content="yes">
    <meta name="apple-mobile-web-app-status-bar-style" content="black-translucent">
    <style type="text/css">
        body {
            margin: 0;
        }
    </style>
```

```
        <link rel='stylesheet' href='style.css' type='text/css'>
        <script src='/static/enchant.js-latest/enchant.js'></script>
        <script src='/code.9leap.js'></script>
        <script src='main.js'></script>
        <title>HelloEnchant</title>
    </head>
    <body>
    </body>
</html>
```

Let's take a look at the new HTML tags we added. The following code sets the character encoding to UTF-8 (unicode), a character encoding that is compatible with practically all characters used in most modern languages.

- `<meta charset="utf-8">`

The following code disables scaling by the user (zoom) to ensure the game always looks correct.

- `<meta name="viewport" content="width=device-width, user-scalable=no">`

The following code sets the display to full screen.

- `<meta name="apple-mobile-web-app-capable" content="yes">`

The following code changes how the status bar is displayed.

- `<meta name="apple-mobile-web-app-status-bar-style" content="black-translucent">`

The following code sets the HTML body margin to 0 to keep things looking the same across browsers.

- `<style type="text/css"> body { margin: 0; } </style>`

We will use this HTML file for all the applications in this book. Other than changing which libraries we import, the only thing we change is the title.

Preview Your Results

As shown in Figure 1-14, when you have finished editing the source code, save your progress by clicking the Run button in the upper-right corner of the screen. If you entered the source code correctly, the bear should skate from left to right.

Figure 1-14. *The display preview*

If the preview looks strange, check your source code to make sure it matches. In particular, be on the lookout for missing semicolons (;), misplaced periods, and misspelled names.

We can print strings to the console, a special output screen just for developers, by using something called log output. It can be used to check the value of variables and the way a program is executing. To print the value of a variable named sum on the log screen, use the notation in Listing 1-21.

Listing 1-21. Showing the Name of a Variable in the Console

```
console.log("Total = " + sum); console.log("sum = " + sum);
```

If you are using Google Chrome as your browser, you can use the following steps to view the output of the log.

1. Open the console by right-clicking the part of the window running the game and select Inspect Element, shown in Figure 1-15.

Figure 1-15. *Choosing Inspect Element from the drop-down menu*

2. The Developer Tools window will open. Click the Console button to display the console. If your application is not working because of JavaScript syntax errors, the error type and line number will be displayed in the console.

Finish Source Code Editing

To finish editing the source code, click the Finish button on the source code editing screen. You will be redirected back to your dashboard.

Executing on Devices and Uploading to 9leap.net

As we stated in the beginning of this chapter, many of the games authored in enchant.js so far have been designed to be played in mobile browsers. Once you have finished coding your game, we recommend checking your source code, testing your game on a mobile device, and, if you are so inclined, sharing your game on 9leap.net.

Source Code Viewing Screen

Open the Source Code View, shown in Figure 1-16, of your own project or sample project by clicking on the name of the project from the dashboard. There, you can view and execute the source code, get URLs to run the code on other devices, create a tag to embed on blogs, and publish the game on 9leap.net. On your dashboard, click HelloEnchant to open the source code view of the project that you just created. In the upper part of the screen, you will find various buttons whose functions are explained in Table 1-4.

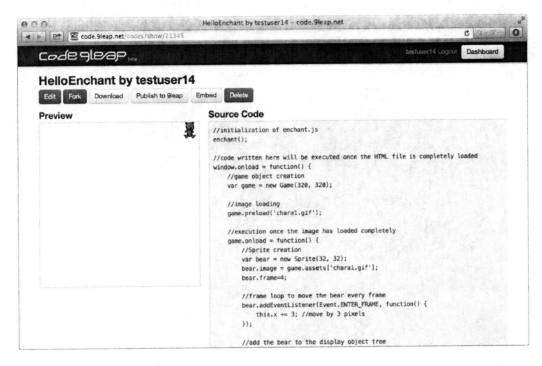

Figure 1-16. *The source code viewing screen*

Table 1-4. *Buttons on the Source Code Viewing Screen*

Edit Button	Return to the source code editing screen to edit.
Fork Button	Start a new project with this source code.
Download Button	Download the source code and resources used by the project to your local hard drive.
Publish to 9leap.net	Share your app on 9leap.net (beta).
Embed Button	Create a tag for embedding the application in a blog, web site, and so on.
Delete Button	Delete this project.

Below these buttons you can see a preview of your application on the left side that is executed automatically when you open the screen. The source code appears on the right.

Execute on Devices

To execute your enchant.js app through code.9leap.net on an iPhone, Android, or other device, perform the following steps.

1. Check the project ID by looking at the URL of the project, as shown in Figure 1-17. In this case, the ID is 21345.

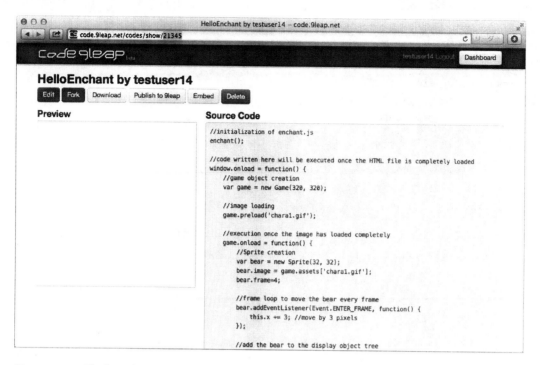

Figure 1-17. *Checking the project ID*

2. Use this ID to create a URL that can be opened on mobile devices. If the URL shown in the window is http://code.9leap.net/codes/show/21345, then the mobile URL will be http://coderun.9leap.net/codes/21345. This example is shown in Figure 1-18.

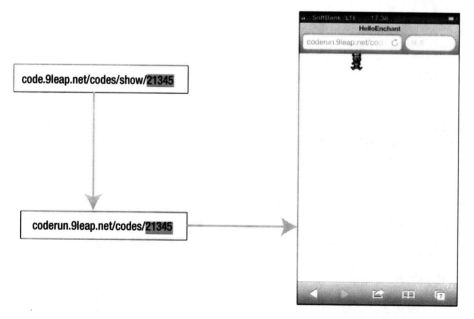

Figure 1-18. *Running code on a device*

Embedding in a Blog

To create a tag to embed your enchant.js app in a blog or on a web site, click the Embed button in the source code view. An embedding tag, shown in Figure 1-19, will appear. Copy and paste this tag into the HTML code of your web site or blog. If you have a simple web site, you can paste the tag directly into a <div> or the <body> tag of your site, but if you use a content management system, like WordPress, you may need to enable HTML editing while writing or editing a new page or post to successfully paste in this tag.

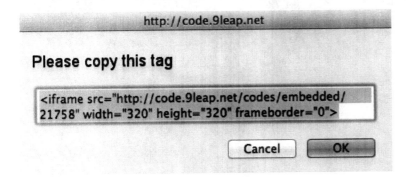

Figure 1-19. *The embedding pop-up*

Submitting to 9leap.net

When your enchant.js app is completed, try sharing it on 9leap.net! You can set it to private mode at first to give yourself a chance to test it before making it public. Follow the steps below to share your application. (As of the writing of this book, the Publish to 9leap button is still being tested.)

1. Click the Download button in the source code viewing screen. Your browser will download the game in a zip file.

2. Go to 9leap.net, shown in Figure 1-20, and log in using your Twitter account. (If you don't have one, you'll need to register one before you can use 9leap.net.) The button might appear in English or Japanese because the site is still in the beta stage.

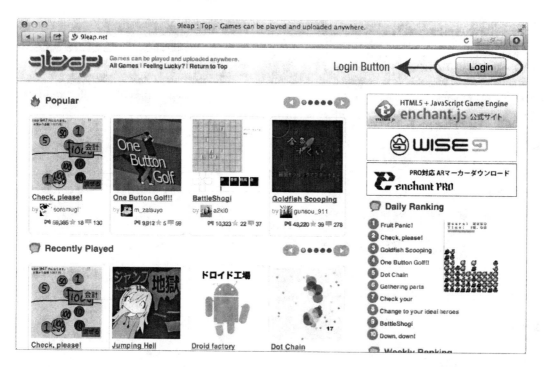

Figure 1-20. *The log-in button on* `9leap.net`

    3.   Click Game Upload/Edit Screen, as shown at the top of the screen in Figure 1-21.

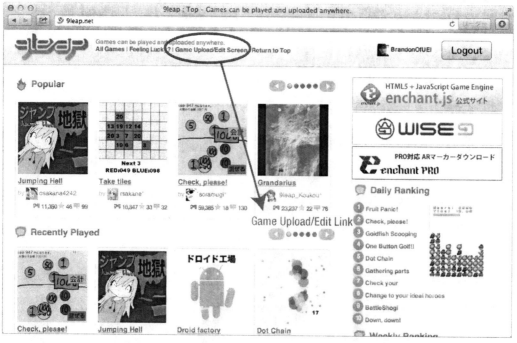

Figure 1-21. *The Game Upload/Edit link*

4. Click on Add New, as shown in Figure 1-22.

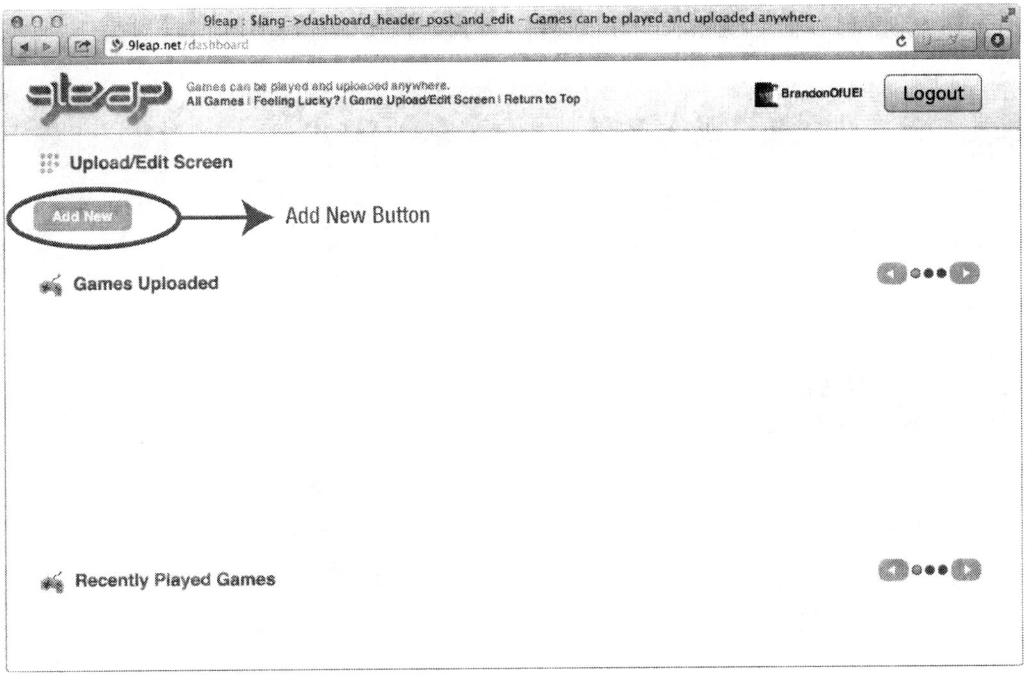

Figure 1-22. *The Add New button*

5. Accept the terms of service, fill in your information, and click Send, as shown in Figure 1-23. This information is used to consider the game for contests on the site.

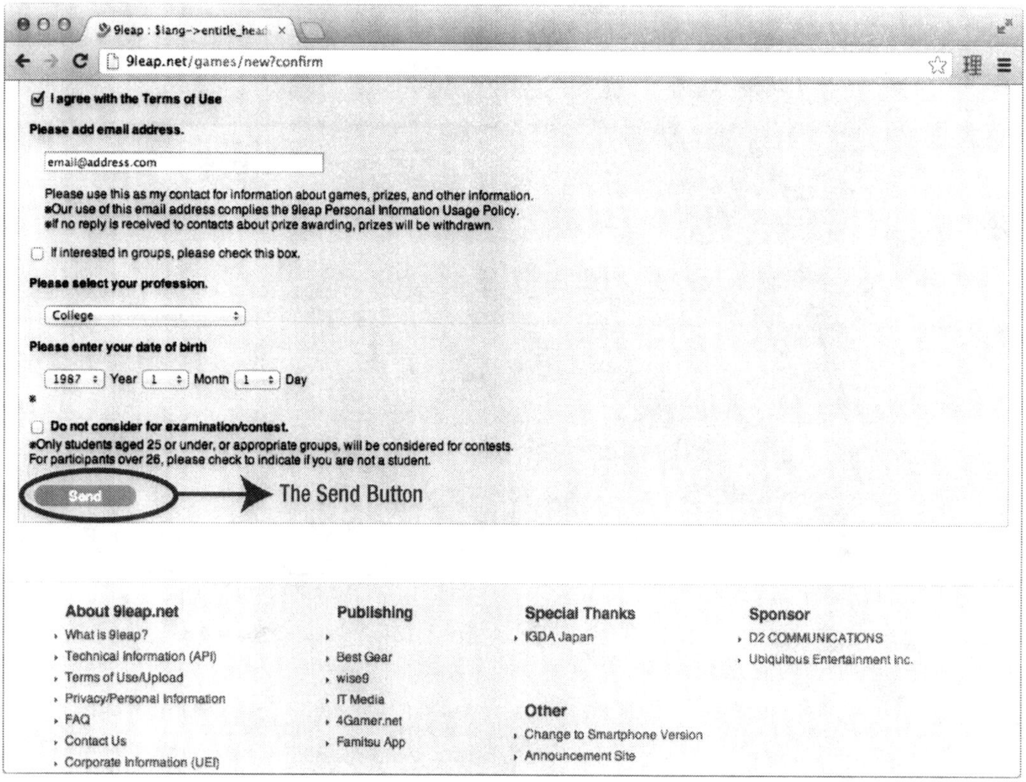

Figure 1-23. *The Send button*

6. Fill in the information for your game in the blanks. These fields are explained in Table 1-5. For the Game File, locate the zip file of your game that was saved from code.9leap.net. You need to include a screenshot, which can be an image file from your game or a screencap. (Please see http://bit.ly/11m6e4 for screencap information for a Mac and http://bit.ly/ZFSdT for a PC.) Make sure to indicate which license you would like to license your game under. When you are finished, click the Post Game button, as shown in Figure 1-24.

Table 1-5. *Game Information Fields*

Game Title	Enter your game's title in 40 characters or less.
Genre	Select a genre for your game.
Game Explanation	Explain the goal of your game and how to play it in 1,000 characters or less.
Game File	A zip file less than 10MB in size containing the game.
Screenshot	Screenshot for your game (less than 1MB - jpg/png/gif).
Runtime Environment	Indicate the compatibility of browsers for your game.
Twitter Settings	Indicate if you would like 9leap to announce your posting of the game on Twitter.
Set as Private	Select this option if you would like your game to be viewable only by you.
Submit for Contests	If there are contests currently being held on 9leap for which your game might be eligible, they will appear here.
Source Code License	If you would like to specify a license under which your game will be protected, specify it here.

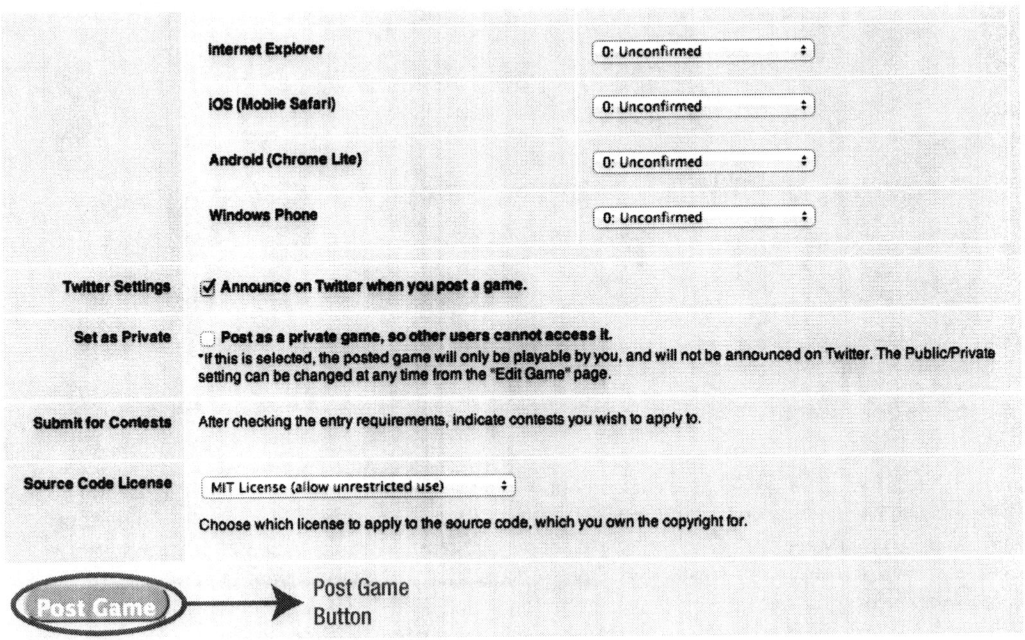

Figure 1-24. *The Upload button*

The private setting can be changed at any time from the game editing settings page.

After you upload your game successfully, the sharing completed screen will be displayed and you can view your game on the Game Upload/Edit Screen. See Figure 1-25.

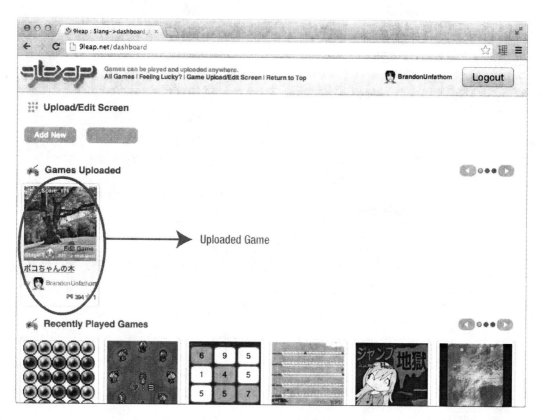

Figure 1-25. Uploaded game appears on the Game Upload/Edit Screen

Conclusion

In this chapter we introduced rudimentary features of enchant.js and showed how an enchant.js game fits into the structure of a web page. We touched on JavaScript, HTML5, and CSS, and how to get started with coding your games on `code.9leap.net`. Finally, we took a look at how to share your games with the enchant.js community on `global.9leap.net`, and how playing games created by other users can give you ideas for your own games.

In the next chapter, we cover the building blocks of JavaScript, which is the language enchant.js is written in. Learning JavaScript will give you the foundation to start creating your own games with enchant.js.

CHAPTER 2

■ ■ ■

JavaScript Basics

As we said in Chapter 1, enchant.js is written in the JavaScript programming language. When you program games in enchant.js, you'll write commands and other code in the JavaScript language, so we need to examine simple JavaScript before diving headfirst into enchant.js games. If you are already familiar with JavaScript, feel free to skip this chapter.

JavaScript is the primary programming language used for scripting on web pages. Unlike most programming languages used to create software applications that must be installed on computers to function, JavaScript code runs on the client web browser. Given that enchant.js and games written using enchant.js are created using JavaScript, it is imperative to understand the fundamental concepts of JavaScript. If you are new to programming, learning these fundamentals will benefit you immensely, as they happen to also be the building blocks of object-oriented languages and are a useful starting point from which to learn other popular programming languages, such as Java and C++.

The grammar of a programming language, or rather, the specific way elements of the language are written, is called syntax. In this chapter, you learn the building blocks of JavaScript, their syntax, and their functions by writing code on the code.9leap.net web site. We'll take you step-by-step through the process and explain each of these building blocks through a series of simple code projects.

Summary List

In this chapter, we'll show you how to do the following:

1. Declare a Variable

2. Assign a Value to a Variable

3. Add Variables

4. Check the Value of a Variable

5. Manipulate a Variable Using Itself

6. Manipulate a Variable Using Incrementation

7. Compare a Variable

8. See How Similar Two Variables Can Be

9. Manipulate a Comparison

10. Implement Logic with the If Statement

11. Create an Object

12. Work Smarter with the While and For Loop Statements

13. Interrupt a Loop with Break

14. Skip a Loop Iteration with Continue

15. Generate Random Numbers

16. Define Scenarios with Switch

17. Store Numbered Data in an Array

18. Store Non-Numbered Data in an Associative Array

19. Save Time with Functions

20. See Where Variables Live

21. Make Object Blueprints with Prototypes

Declare a Variable

Variables are containers for values and in most cases can be updated at any time with a new value, hence their name. Their values "vary," so they are "variable." The benefit of using variables over explicit values is due to the dynamic nature of a variable. If you include a variable in a calculation, and then later change the value of that variable, the next time you perform the same calculation the new value will be used.

To use a variable, you must first declare it with the var statement, which tells the application to reserve a spot in memory for the variable. At the end of any single statement in JavaScript, you must include a semicolon (;).

To declare three variables with the names num0, num1, and sum, do the following:

1. Go to http://code.9leap.net and log in or sign up if you don't already have an account.

2. Go to http://code.9leap.net/codes/show/26854 and fork the Blank JavaScript Template by clicking the Fork button.

3. Change the title of the project by modifying the field directly to the right of the code.9leap logo in the upper-left corner of the screen. Choose something appropriate such as "Declare a Variable." (For all future examples forking this code, please change the title in this manner to keep track of your individual projects.)

4. Type in the code shown in Listing 2-1.

    Listing 2-1. Declaring a Variable

    ```
    var num0;
    var num1;
    var sum;
    ```

Naming Variables

You can use the following characters in variable names:

- letters (A–Z, a–z)

- numbers (but not as the first character of a variable name)

- underscores (_)

Table 2-1 shows reserved words in JavaScript that cannot be used as variable names.

Table 2-1. *Reserved Words in JavaScript*

break	do	if	switch	typeof
case	else	in	this	var
catch	false	instanceof	throw	void
continue	finally	new	true	while
default	for	null	try	with
delete	function	return		

Table 2-2 shows words that currently are not used, but have a high probability of being used in the future. We recommend avoiding them when naming your variables.

Table 2-2. *Words Reserved for Future Use*

abstract	double	goto	native	static
boolean	enum	implements	package	super
byte	export	import	private	synchronized
char	extends	int	protected	throws
class	final	interface	public	transient
const	float	long	short	volatile
debugger				

You cannot use any other word that is predefined for use in JavaScript, such as String, true, and so on. For a complete list, please see www.javascripter.net/faq/reserved.htm.

Assign a Value to a Variable

Once a variable has been declared, a value can be assigned to it. To assign values to num0 and num1, do the following:

1. Below the Listing 2-1 code you entered, type in the code shown in Listing 2-2.

    Listing 2-2. Assigning Values to Variables

    ```
    num0 = 100;
    num1 = 200;
    ```

■ **Note**   Variables can be declared and assigned a value at the same time by using

```
var num3 = 400;
```

Add Variables

Variables can be used in place of numbers for arithmetic. A variable's current value will be used for the calculation if arithmetic is performed using a variable. To add num0 and num1 and assign the result to sum, do the following:

1. Below the Listing 2-2 code you entered, type in the code shown in Listing 2-3.

    Listing 2-3. Adding Variables

    ```
    sum = num0 + num1;
    ```

Basic Arithmetic Operators

You are not limited to just adding variables or numbers. All the basic arithmetic operations can be performed. Table 2-3 shows the basic operators.

Table 2-3. *Basic Arithmetic Operators*

Operator	Description	Example
+	Addition	a + b (add a and b)
–	Subtraction	a – b (subtract b from a)
*	Multiplication	a * b (multiply a and b)
/	Division	a / b (divide a by b)
%	Remainder	a % b (the remainder of a divided by b. In other words, 7 % 4 = 3 because 4 goes into 7 one time, with a remainder of three.)

The operators possess a priority: multiplication and division take place first, before addition and subtraction. To change the order of precedence, which might be useful if you want to calculate specific sections of a calculation before others, use parentheses, as seen in Listing 2-4. You do not need to copy this code. It is just for reference.

Listing 2-4. Changing the Order of Operations with Parentheses

```
var result0 = 1 + 2 * 3;        //result0 will be 7
var result1 = (1 + 2) * 3;      //result1 will be 9
```

Check the Value of a Variable

To see the value of sum, do the following:

1. Below your current code, type in the code shown in Listing 2-5. The document.write() command tells the program to display whatever is within the parentheses on-screen, and uses the plus sign to combine, or concatenate, values together to display a final result. Commands like this are called *methods*, and can be identified by the parentheses at the end of the method name. The period before write indicates that it is a method of the document object, a predefined set of code allowing JavaScript to have access to the browser window. We'll cover objects in more detail later.

Listing 2-5. Displaying the Value of Sum on the Screen

```
document.write("Total amount = " + sum);
```

2. Click the Run button. (We will refer to this simply as Run hereafter.) The preview area should show "Total amount = 300".

If you would like to check your code against a finished example, you can find one at
`http://code.9leap.net/codes/show/19823`.

Data Types

Why do we have to put quotes around what we place inside of `document.write()` in Listing 2-5? This is because `document.write()` accepts only values that are a string. A string, used to store strings of text characters, is one of the five basic, or primitive, data types in JavaScript. Three of those data types-number, string, and Boolean-are used to store data, while the other two are used to designate the current state of a variable. Table 2-4 shows the five data types.

Table 2-4. Basic Data Types

Type	Assigned Value	Usage Example

Number	Base 10
	Base 8 (0 appended to beginning of value)
	Base 16 (0x appended to beginning of value)
	Floating point, base 10 (using a period [.])
	Floating point, exponent (using a period[.] and E)
		var num = 10;
		var num = 011;
		var num = 0x9A;
		var fnum = 3.1415;
		var fnum = -3.1E12;

Boolean	true or false	var flag = true;
String	String surrounded by double or single quotations	var str = "character string"; var str = 'character string';
null	The object is known to exist, but has no value	var obj = null;
undefined	The object does not exist, does not return a value, or has not been initialized	

In addition to the basic data types, there are complex data types in JavaScript:

- *Object*: Objects are a set of multiple basic data types and/or other objects, usually either predefined or defined by the developer. If you were to create a bowling game, you would most likely have multiple objects representing bowling pins, and another object representing the bowling ball.

- *Array*: An array is a set of indexed and ordered data. In the bowling game example, your bowling pin objects could all be stored inside a single array. Each item added to the array is assigned a number, starting with 0, and increased by 1 with each item added to the array.

- *Associative array*: An associative array is a set of named data joined together in no particular order. Unlike a regular array, associative arrays can pair together an item with any other value or item. Imagine for a moment that our bowling game is a 3-D game, and that there are several lights suspended above the bowling pins. An associative array could be used to link together each bowling pin to a specific light.

- *Function*: Functions execute a defined computation or set of code. In the bowling game example, a function could be used to cause the bowling pin to tip over if the bowling ball comes in contact with the pin.

We'll cover the complex data types in more detail later.

■ **Note** In programming languages like C/C++ and Java, variables have static data types (such as integer or string), and you cannot assign a value of one data type to a variable of a different data type. In other words, if you have an integer variable, you cannot assign a string of characters to that variable.

In JavaScript, this is not the case. A value of any data type can be assigned to a variable, and a variable of a completely different data type can later be reassigned to the same variable. A variable of name foo could be assigned a number value with foo = 10; and then the very next line could state foo = "bar"; to assign a string value to the same variable. This flexibility is a major benefit in JavaScript, but the drawback is that sometimes you have to take extra care when performing calculations. We'll see examples of this later on.

Manipulate a Variable Using Itself

Many games contain a score that is constantly updated when a player gets points. To update this score, the variable containing it must be increased. Do the following to see how:

1. Clear the code you wrote up to Listing 2-5.

2. Type in the code shown in Listing 2-6.

   Listing 2-6. Manipulating a Variable by Referencing Itself

   ```
   var score = 10;
   score = score + 20;
   document.write(score);
   ```

3. Click Run. The preview screen should show "30."

4. Replace score = score + 20; with score += 20;

5. Click Run again. The result is the same. Step 4 uses an abbreviated form of the self-referencing operation called a compound assignment operator.

Compound Assignment Operators

Compound assignment operators are operators that perform a value assignment to a variable along with another operation simultaneously. Table 2-5 shows these useful operators.

Table 2-5. *Compound Assignment Operators*

Operator	Description	Example
+=	Addition	a += 10 (equivalent to a = a + 10)
−=	Subtraction	a −= 10 (equivalent to a = a − 10)
*=	Multiplication	a *= 10 (equivalent to a = a * 10)
/=	Division	a /= 10 (equivalent to a = a / 10)
%=	Remainder	a %= 10 (equivalent to a = a % 10)

Manipulate a Variable Using Incrementation

When a variable needs to be increased by a value of 1, an even more abbreviated operator can be used. Do the following to see it in action:

1. Clear your current code.

2. Type in the code in Listing 2-7.

   Listing 2-7. Declaring and Incrementing a Variable

   ```
   var num = 1;
   num++;
   document.write(num);
   ```

3. Click Run. The preview screen should show "2," showing that ++ increases the value of num by 1.

4. Clear your current code.

5. Type in Listing 2-8.

   Listing 2-8. Incrementing a Variable within a Statement

   ```
   var num = 1;
   document.write(num++);
   num = 1;
   document.write(++num);
   ```

6. Click Run. The screen first shows "1" and then "2." When inside a statement like document. write(), if the increment operator (++) is after the variable, the document.write() statement will be executed first, and if the operator appears before the variable, the operator will be executed before document.write().

▧ **Note** The opposite of the increment operator is the decrement operator (--). The decrement operator works in the exact same way as the increment operator, except that it subtracts one from whichever variable it is attached to.

Compare a Variable

JavaScript contains commands called *relational operators* that compare two values and return a Boolean value of true or false, depending on the result. Do the following to see them in action:

1. Clear your current code.

2. Type in the code in Listing 2-9.

    Listing 2-9. Comparing Values

    ```
    var num0 = 4;
    var num1 = 7;
    document.write(num0 >= num1);
    document.write(num0 < num1);
    document.write(num0 === num1);
    ```

3. Click Run. The screen first shows false, as 4 is not greater than or equal to 7; shows true, as 4 is less than 7; and shows false again, as 4 is not equal to 7.

Table 2-6 shows the useable relational operators.

Table 2-6. *Relational Operators*

Operator	Description	Example
==	Equivalent	a == b
===	Strictly equivalent	a === b
!=	Inequivalent	a != b
!==	Strictly inequivalent	a !== b
>	Greater than	a > b
>=	Greater than or equal to	a >= b
<	Less than	a < b
<=	Less than or equal to	a <= b

See How Similar Two Values Can Be

See how the equivalent (==) and strictly equivalent (===) relational operators differ by doing the following:

1. Clear your current code.

2. Type in the code in Listing 2-10.

    Listing 2-10. Differing Equivalent Operators

    ```
    var num0 = 4;
    var num1 = "4";
    document.write(num0 == num1);
    document.write(num0 === num1);
    ```

3. Click Run. The screen first shows true, as the == sign temporarily converts all values to strings if one of the values being compared is a string. This is called *type conversion*. The screen then shows false, as the === sign does not perform type conversion. To evaluate as the same, compared values must be of the same data type.

Note The opposite of the equivalent operators are the inequivalent operators (!= and !==), which perform almost the exact same operation. However, the != operator performs type conversion and the !== operator does not.

Manipulate a Comparison

Sometimes you'll want to manipulate how a comparison resolves (true/false). To see how these comparisons can be manipulated, do the following:

4. Clear your code.

5. Type in the code in Listing 2-11.

   Listing 2-11. Manipulating Comparisons

   ```
   document.write(!(4 > 3));
   document.write((4 < 7) && (5 < 13));
   document.write((4 > 5) || (4 < 5));
   ```

6. Click Run.

The screen will first say false because the statement (4 > 3) resolves to true, and the ! logical operator reverses the Boolean statement (true/false) after it, making it false. The screen then lists true because both (4 < 7) and (5 < 13) evaluate to true. The && (and) logical operator returns true only if both statements around it are true. Finally, the screen shows true again, because out of (4 > 5) and (4 < 5), one of them is true. The || (or) operator resolves as true if at least one of the statements is true. Table 2-7 shows the logical operators.

Table 2-7. Logical Operators

Operator	Description	Example
!	false if a is true, true if a is false	!a
&&	true if both a and b are true, otherwise false	a&&b
||	true if a or b is true, otherwise false	a||b

Implement Logic with the If Statement

Sometimes we want to perform specific actions in our code if and only if a certain condition is met. Do the following to see how:

1. Clear your current code.

2. Type in the code in Listing 2-12.

Listing 2-12. Implementing Logic with the If Statement

```
var num0 = 4;
var num1 = 8;
if (num0 >= num1) {
    document.write(num0 + " is greater than or equal to " + num1 + ".");
}
else if (num0 < num1) {
    document.write(num0 + " is less than " + num1 + ".");
}
```

3. Click Run. The screen will display "4 is less than 8." Change the values of num0 and num1 to see how you can change the results. The else if() statement will be evaluated only if the first if statement evaluates as false (num0 >= num1 returns false).

Create an Object

An object is a structure that can contain its own variables (called *properties*), and methods. These are called *instance properties* and *instance methods* when they belong to an object. To create an object that will enable you to get the current date, do the following:

1. Clear your code.

2. Type in the code in Listing 2-13. This code creates a variable as an instance of an object called the Date object, which contains methods that can give us information about the current date. The new Date() part of the code is called the *constructor* of the Date object, and by assigning it to a variable, you create the object.

Listing 2-13. Creating the Date Object

```
var date = new Date();
```

3. Type in the code in Listing 2-14. The methods of the date object return information about the year, month, or day of the current date. When getMonth() is called, 1 is added to the result because getMonth() counts January as 0, February as 1, and so on. Table 2-8 shows the methods that can be used with the Date object.

Listing 2-14. Assigning Date Information to Variables

```
var y = date.getFullYear();
var m = date.getMonth() + 1;
var d = date.getDate();
```

Table 2-8. *Methods of the Date Object*

Method	Effect	Return Value
getFullYear()	Returns the four-digit Gregorian calendar year	{Number} 4-digit Gregorian calendar year
getMonth()	Returns the month - 1 (this is because it is an array reference)	{Number} Month - 1
getDate()	Returns the day	{Number} Day
getDay()	Returns the day of the week	{Number} Day of the week
getHours()	Returns the hour	{Number} Hour
getMinutes()	Returns the minute	{Number} Minute
getSeconds()	Returns the second	{Number} Second
getMilliseconds()	Returns the millisecond	{Number} Millisecond

4. Type in the code in Listing 2-15. You are concatenating multiple strings and values of the month, day, and year variables together into a single variable, text.

Listing 2-15. Creating a String and Displaying It

```
var text = "The date is " + m + "/" + d + "/" + y;
document.write(text);
```

5. Click Run. A string is displayed onscreen showing the current date. If you run into problems, you can view the full code sample at http://code.9leap.net/codes/show/19827.

The Date object is just one of the many objects that come predefined with JavaScript. Table 2-9 contains some of the main objects bundled with JavaScript.

Table 2-9. *Main Objects Included with JavaScript*

Object Name	Object Description
window	Browser window
document	Web page in a browser
frame	Frame within a web page
history	Browser history
location	Current page location
anchor	HTML hyperlink
applet	Embedded program in a web page
area	Clickable area on an image
form	Web form
image	Image on a web page
layer	Layers for transparent elements
link	Link to external style resource

(*continued*)

Table 2-9. (*continued*)

Object Name	Object Description
button	Clickable button
checkbox	Markable check box
fileupload	Dialog box for file upload
hidden	Conceals passwords
password	Accepts a password
radio	Markable radio button
reset	Clears choices in a form
text	Single line of text
linkarea	Text area
select	Selection on a drop-down menu
Array	Array of values
Boolean	Boolean value (`true`/`false`)
Date	Stores a date
Event	Occurs with an event (such as a click)
Function	Function (method)
Math	Numerical calculations
Navigator	Browser information
Number	Stores a number
Object	Stores code elements
RegExp	Regular expression
String	String of characters

This large list of objects might seem daunting at first, but it's only meant as a quick reference. If you'd like to learn more, see the section on "Predefined Core Objects" in the Mozilla Developer Network's JavaScript guide at `https://developer.mozilla.org/en-US/docs/JavaScript/Guide/Predefined_Core_Objects`. It's a great resource on the basic core objects of JavaScript and their uses.

Note   If you are familiar with object-oriented languages such as C/C++ or Java, you might be familiar with the concept of *class*. In these languages, classes act as predefined templates for objects. Properties and methods can be defined for a given class, and then all objects created from that class will inherit those properties and methods.

In JavaScript, the concept of class technically does not exist and is replaced by the concept of *prototypes*. A prototype is a specially designated object for which properties and methods can be defined. When new objects are created, they can be created from a prototype and will have the same properties and methods of that prototype.

The concept of class and prototype might seem similar at first, but they are different in their restrictions. We will not discuss class-based vs. prototype-based programming in detail, but the main difference is objects created from prototypes can override predefined prototype functions with their own function definitions, while objects created as part of a class are generally unable to do so.

Work Smarter with the While and For Loop Statements

Repetition makes your coding life easier because there are many cases where a program can be easily engineered to perform repetitive tasks for you. Let's imagine we need to devise a way to add together all the numbers between 1 and 1000 and assign that value to a variable (int). If we were to manually add every single number between 1 and 100, we'd end up with code that would look something like the code in Listing 2-16.

Listing 2-16. An Impractical Way to Add Sequential Numbers

```
int num = 1 + 2 + 3 + 4 + 5 + 6 + 7 + 8 + 9 + 10 + 11 + 12 + 13 + 14 + 15 + 16 + 17 + 18 + 19 + 20
+ 21 + 22 + 23 + 24 + 25 + 26 + 27 + 28 + 29 + 30 + 31 + 32 + 33 + 34 + 35 + 36 + 37 + 38 + 39 + 40
+ 41 + 42 + 43 + 44 + 45 + 46 + 47 + 48 + 49 + 50 + 51 + 52 + 53 + 54 + 55 + 56 + 57 + 58 + 59 + 60
+ 61 + 62 + 63 + 64 + 65 + 66 + 67 + 68 + 69 + 70 + 71 + 72 + 73 + 74 + 75 + 76 + 77 + 78 + 79 + 80
+ 81 + 82 + 83 + 84 + 85 + 86 + 87 + 88 + 89 + 90 + 91 + 92 + 93 + 94 + 95 + 96 + 97 + 98 + 99 + 100;
```

Ouch. That doesn't look like a very practical way to spend your time, does it? To speed things up, we can use loop statements to perform this repetitive calculation for us. To see this in action, do the following steps:

1. Clear your code.

2. Type in the code in Listing 2-17 to first create a variable, i, which will be used to control the loop (in other words, the control variable), and then create two other variables to store the results from the upcoming loops.

   Listing 2-17. Creating Variables

   ```
   var i;
   var sumFor;
   var sumWhile;
   ```

3. Create a while loop to add together all numbers from 1 to 100 by typing in the code in Listing 2-18 after your current code. First, you must give sumWhile a value of 0 because you will be using a self-referencing operator (+=) in your code, so it must have a value before you begin. Next, you give i a value of 1. This number represents both the first time through the while loop, and the first number to be added to sumWhile. Finally, you enter the while loop. At the beginning of the while loop, the program will check to see if i has a current value equal to or less than 100. If it does, it will move into the loop, add the current value of i to sumWhile, and then add one to i. The loop will then check again to see if i is less than or equal to 100 and start again. This will continue repeatedly until the last value, 100, is added to sumWhile.

   Listing 2-18. The While Loop

   ```
   sumWhile = 0;
   i = 1;
   while (i <= 100) {
           sumWhile += i;
           i++;
   }
   document.write("The result using a while loop: " + sumWhile + "<BR />");
   ```

■ **Note** The "<BR />" in the `document.write()` method is an HTML tag (the name of an HTML element surrounded by brackets, specifying an element of a web page to be inserted) that tells the system to move down a line before displaying more text.

---

4. Click Run. The screen will display the result of 5050.

5. Now do the same thing with a different kind of loop, the for loop, by typing in the code in Listing 2-19 below your current code. The `for` loop has three statements at the beginning of it. The first (`i = 1;`) declares and creates a variable to control the loop. The second one (`i <= 100;`) is checked before the for loop is run or rerun, exactly the same as the statement at the beginning of the `while` loop. Finally, the last statement (`i++`) is run when a `for` loop completes, before the second statement is checked against for a rerun.

    Listing 2-19. The For Loop

    ```
    sumFor = 0;
    for (i = 1; i <= 100; i++) {
            sumFor += i;
    }
    document.write("The result using a for loop: " + sumFor + "<BR />");
    ```

6. Click Run. The screen will display 5050 twice, as both loops calculate the same thing. If you run into problems, you can check your code against the full code sample at `http://code.9leap.net/codes/show/19828`.

■ **Tip** If a `for` statement has only one command, as does the one in Listing 2-19, the curly braces are not necessary. For instance, the `for` loop in the listing could be rewritten as

```
for (i = 1; i <= 1000; i++) sumFor = sumFor + i;
```

Interrupt a Loop with Break

Occasionally, in the middle of a loop's execution, we want to stop the processing of the code in that loop and continue processing code past the end of the loop. This is easily accomplished with the break statement, which breaks the current processing out of the loop, even if the loop's condition is still fulfilled. To see it in action, do the following:

1. Clear your code.

2. Type in the code in Listing 2-20.

    Listing 2-20. Breaking Out of a Loop

    ```
    var sumWhile = 0;
    var i = 1;
    while (true) {
        sumWhile += i;
    ```

```
        i++;
        if (i > 100) break;
    }
    document.write(sumWhile);
```

3. Click Run. The result is the same as before. When i is equal to 100, it gets added to sumWhile, becomes 101, and then because it is greater than 100, the while loop stops.

Skip a Loop Iteration with Continue

On other occasions, you might want to skip the remaining code in a loop and start it again. As long as the conditional expression of a for or while loop is fulfilled, this can be done with the continue statement. When this statement is issued, the next iteration of the loop's code is immediately started. As usual in a for loop, when returning to the beginning of the loop code, the increment/decrement expression of the for loop get executed. Do the following steps to try this out by making a program that calculates only the even numbers from 0 to 100:

1. Clear your code.

2. Type in the code from Listing 2-21. The line if (i % 2 != 0) continue; says if the remainder after dividing i by 2 is not 0 (if i is odd), skip the remaining code in the current for loop iteration and begin the next for loop iteration immediately.

Listing 2-21. Using Continue to Skip Odd Numbers

```
var sumFor = 0;
for (i = 1; i <= 100; i++) {
    if (i % 2 != 0) continue;
    sumFor = sumFor + i;
}
document.write("The sum of all even numbers up to 100 is " + sumFor);
```

3. Click Run. A result of 2550 is displayed.

Generate Random Numbers

If you want enemy characters to appear randomly in your game or if you want to create a game that tells you your fortune for the day and randomly assigns you a "luckiness" value, you need to be able to create random numbers. Do the following to see how it works for a fortune-telling game:

1. Clear your code.

2. Type in the code in Listing 2-22 to create variables and assign a random number to num.

Listing 2-22. Creating Variables for the Fortune-Telling Game

```
var num;
var text = "";
num = Math.floor(Math.random() * 4);
```

`Math.random()` returns a value from 0 (inclusive) up to 1 (exclusive – not including 1). By multiplying this by 4, you get a value from 0 up to, but not including, 4. The `floor()` method of the `Math` object rounds down whatever is in its parentheses. Thus, the code you just wrote will return 0, 1, 2, or 3, randomly.

3.   Create the fortune-telling game using your random variable by typing in the code in Listing 2-23 below your current code.

Listing 2-23. Fortune Telling with the If Statement

```
if (num===0) {
    text = "Super Lucky";
} else if (num===1) {
    text = "So-so Luck";
} else if (num===2) {
    text = "Minor Luck";
} else {
    text = "Bad Luck";
}
document.write("Your fortune: " + text);
```

Here, you are assigning a value to `text` depending on the value of `num` and then outputting the result.

4.   Click Run. You randomly get a response for your current level of "luckiness."

Define Scenarios with Switch

In the last code example, several `if` statements were used to determine what value should have been assigned to `text`. However, there is an easier way to make this work, without all the `if` statements. Do the following to see how:

1.   Delete the `document.write()` statement and all `if` statements. Your code should look as it does in Listing 2-24.

Listing 2-24. Setting Up for the Switch Example

```
var num;
var text = "";
num = Math.floor(Math.random() * 4);
```

2.   Add the switch statement by typing in the code in Listing 2-25 below your current code.

Listing 2-25. The Fortune-Telling Switch Statement

```
switch (num) {
        case 0:
                textSwitch = "Excellent Luck";
                break;
        case 1:
                textSwitch = "Moderate Luck";
                break;
        case 2:
                textSwitch = "Small Luck";
                break;
```

```
default:
        textSwitch = "Bad Luck";
        break;
}
```

The switch statement takes whatever value is in its parenthesis, finds the case that matches that number, and then executes the code beneath it. If there is no break statement in the current case, the switch statement will continue executing code from the next case and so on, until either a break statement is encountered or the end of the switch statement is reached. The default case is executed if no matches are found.

3. Click Run. You will get a randomly generated fortune.

Store Numbered Data in an Array

Arrays are used to keep track of sets of data, which are necessary when dealing with maps, strings (arrays of text characters), and more. Do the following to see how a set of numerically indexed (numbered) data can be created in an array:

1. Clear your code.

2. Create an array to represent a collection of three devices by typing in the code in Listing 2-26.

Listing 2-26. Creating an Array of Devices

```
var array = new Array(3);
array[0] = "iPhone";
array[1] = "Android";
array[2] = "Computer";
```

Just like when we created an instance of the Date object, you use a constructor to create an array (new Array(3)). The Array(3) tells the program to create an array with 3 spaces.

3. Create a string to save parts of the array into it, and then iterate through the array, adding all of the array elements to the string before displaying it. Listing 2-27 shows how to do this.

Listing 2-27. Iterating Through an Array

```
var text = "";
for (var i = 0; i < array.length; i++) {
    text += array[i] + "<BR />";
}
document.write(text);
```

Notice how the compound assignment operator += can be used to add characters to the end of a string. Using a for loop allows you to go through all of the elements in an array automatically.

4. Click Run. The screen will display the three elements in the array.

■ **Note**   You do not need to specify the array to be larger to add more items to the array. For example, typing in array[3]="iPad"; in the example above will not cause an error.

Methods of the Array Object

In the previous example you created an array object. That object comes with several methods that can be executed on it. For instance, if you were to type in `array.push("Galaxy");` at the end of your code, it would have added "Galaxy" to the array at whichever position was after the last item in the array. Table 2-10 provides a summary of the array object methods.

Table 2-10. *Methods of the Array Object*

Category	Code	Effect
Add Elements	push(element)	Adds an element to the end of the array.
	unshift(element)	Adds an element to the beginning of the array.
Remove Elements	pop()	Removes the element at the end of the array.
	shift()	Removes the element at the beginning of the array.
Sort Elements	sort()	Sorts the elements of the array in ascending order.
	reverse()	Sorts the elements of the array in reverse order.
Extract Elements	slice(start,end)	Extracts the elements within a specified start and end position and creates a new array with them.
	slice(start)	Extracts the elements from a specified starting position to the end of the array and creates a new array with them.

Store Non-Numbered Data in an Associative Array

What if you want to store a color for each of the devices in the array you just made? To do this, you need to use an associative array instead of a regular array. Do the following to make an associative array:

1. Clear your code.

2. Create your associative array by typing in the code in Listing 2-28.

    Listing 2-28. Creating an Associative Array

    ```
    var obj = new Object();
    obj["iPhone"]    = "White";
    obj["Android"]   = "Black";
    obj["Computer"]  = "Silver";
    ```

Associative arrays are not stored as array objects in JavaScript because all array objects are indexed, containing one key value (starting from 0) and one paired value for each entity in the array. Here, we use the ability of objects in JavaScript to be an array of values to link together the strings of device names and colors.

3. Create a string, add the associative array objects, and then display the string by typing in the code in Listing 2-29.

    Listing 2-29. Manually Iterating Through the Associative Array

    ```
    var textObj = "";
    textObj += "The iPhone is " + obj["iPhone"] + ".<BR />";
    textObj += "The Android is " + obj["Android"] + ".<BR />";
    ```

```
    textObj += "The Computer is " + obj["Computer"] + ".<BR />";
    document.write(textObj);
```

4. Click Run. The list of colors of the devices are displayed on the screen.

Because object arrays are not indexed in the same way as standard arrays, they cannot be iterated through with a simple `for` loop.

Save Time with Functions

You've seen objects that come with their own functions such as arrays, but if you're planning on doing almost anything that requires you to type the same code multiple times, you can define your own functions to save you time. Do the following to see how:

1. Clear your code.

2. Define a function that accepts an argument (whatever is passed in parentheses), and then writes it on the screen after "I will buy the," by typing in the code in Listing 2-30.

    Listing 2-30. Defining the buy() Function

    ```
    function buy(device) {
        document.write("I will buy the " + device + ".<BR />");
    }
    ```

3. Call the function using "iPhone" and "Android" as arguments by typing in the code in Listing 2-31.

    Listing 2-31. Calling the Function

    ```
    buy("iPhone");
    buy("Android");
    ```

4. Click Run. The screen will display the "I will buy" line twice because you called the function twice.

See Where Variables Live

I want you to imagine for a moment that a program you're going to write takes place in a medieval kingdom, with several villages and one castle. For explanatory purposes, imagine the king of this kingdom is named Bob. Throughout the kingdom, if someone talks about Bob, everyone knows that they are talking about the king. However, what if, in a given village, there is also someone else named Bob? Inside that village, people might refer to the local resident Bob as "our Bob," but in the castle if someone refers to "Bob" it's likely everyone will assume the person in question is the king.

This is, in essence, the concept of scope. It refers to the visibility of a variable within a program. In other words, scope is the context for a variable. To see how this works, do the following:

1. Clear your code.

2. Create a variable representing King Bob and assign him a value of 39 to represent his age by typing in the code in Listing 2-32. Because he is the ruler of the kingdom, we will create him as a variable at the beginning of the program, giving him a global scope. This means that if you type "bob" anywhere in the program, the program will know you mean King Bob.

Listing 2-32. Making King Bob

```
var bob = 39;
```

3. Create a function that creates a variable representing a random Bob in one of the kingdom's villages, assign him a random age between 10 and 50, and then increase that age by one to simulate the villager Bob celebrating his birthday, before displaying that Bob's age on the screen, by typing in the code in Listing 2-33.

Listing 2-33. Creating a Function to Create a Random Bob

```
function villager() {
        var bob = Math.floor(Math.random() * 50 + 10);
        this.bob += 1;
        document.write("King Bob's age is " + bob + ".<BR />");
        document.write("Villager Bob, this Bob, is " + this.bob + ".");
}
```

Notice that when you refer to the Bob inside a function, you use this.bob to specify you mean the one inside the function. To explain the visibility of villager Bob, we say he has function scope, instead of global scope like King Bob.

4. Call the villager function by typing in the code in Listing 2-34 below your current code.

Listing 2-34. Calling the Villager Function

```
Villager();
```

5. Click Run to see the result. You will see King Bob's age of 39, and then a random age for villager Bob.

■ **Note**   You cannot reference variables created within a function outside of that function. This is the limitation of function scope. For example, we could not type this.bob outside the function to refer to villager Bob. Outside of villager(), the only Bob we can see or interact with is King Bob.

Make Object Blueprints with Prototypes

Prototypes essentially are a set of blueprints that can be used to create objects. By creating a prototype with properties and methods, we can easily create new objects equipped with the same properties and methods specified in the prototype. To create and use a software prototype that contains a name and a programming language, do the following:

1. Clear your code.

2. Create the prototype first as a function, and then add properties by typing in the code in Listing 2-35.

Listing 2-35. Creating the Prototype and Properties

```
function Software() {
}

Software.prototype.name     = "";
Software.prototype.language = "";
```

3. Create a function for the prototype that displays information about it by typing in the code in Listing 2-36.

Listing 2-36. Creating The Prototype Function

```
Software.prototype.output = function() {
    document.write(this.name + " is written in " + this.language + "<BR />");
};
```

4. Type in the code in Listing 2-37 to create a new object, accounting, as an instance of the Software prototype; specify values for its properties; and then call its function to display information on the screen.

Listing 2-37. Creating the Accounting Object

```
var accounting = new Software();

accounting.name     = "Spreadsheet Master";
accounting.language = "Java";

accounting.output();
```

5. Click Run. You'll see a message saying that Spreadsheet Master is written in Java.

6. Try creating another object below the accounting object and call the output() function. If you run into trouble, check http://code.9leap.net/codes/show/19835 for a working example.

■ **Note**   Using the preceding code as an example, with accounting as the name of an object, you can add properties at any time to this object by typing something like accounting.secondLanguage = "C++";. Here, secondLanguage has not been declared with var or anything before. It is an on-the-fly declaration. Functions can also be added to the object in a similar manner with accounting.showLanguage = function() {document.write(this.language)};.

Conclusion

Congratulations! If you've read through this section and worked with the example code on code.9leap.net, you should now have an understanding of variables, operators, strings, arrays, functions, and prototypes. These are the building blocks of JavaScript as well as many object-oriented languages in current use today. Understanding these basics gives you the foundation you need to learn how to code your own HTML5 games in enchant.js.

In Chapter 3, we delve into the enchant.js library and learn about sprites, scenes, labels, surfaces, and more. These are the basic features that enchant.js provides. As we progress through Chapter 3 and on into Chapter 4, you'll begin to see how these features come together into creating a game.

■ ■ ■

Basic Features of enchant.js

Now that you are familiar with the basics of JavaScript, you should have a much better understanding of how the elements of enchant.js interact and why the elements are written in specific ways. In this chapter, we start with the basic concepts of enchant.js you need to know to start creating games, and then we explore projects that integrate those concepts. We cover inheritance and the display object tree, which are two elements that exist for every enchant.js game, and then we cover labels, sprites, surfaces, touch events, and screen-based interface elements. We use code.9leap.net extensively for the exercises. Once you reach the end of this chapter, you will have a fundamental knowledge of a game's primary components and how to create them.

Summary List

1. Inheritance
2. Seeing Elements of a Game
3. Creating Labels
4. Creating Sprites
5. Drawing a Map with a Surface
6. Using Touch to Interact
7. Using D-Pads to Interact

Inheritance

In object-oriented programming, *inheritance* is a relationship that categorizes one object as a member of a larger category. To better understand this, think of an apple. An apple is a fruit, and to borrow terminology from object-oriented programming, we could say that it inherits the qualities of a fruit. For example, apples contain seeds just like all other fruits. This is analogous to inheritance in object-oriented programming.

One example of an object that can inherit and be inherited is a *node*. Each individual item in a game is called a node. Figure 3-1 shows different types of nodes and how they are classified.

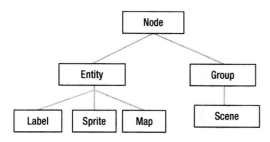

Figure 3-1. *Categorization of Nodes*

Each item in the figure has its own functions and properties. In addition, each item also has the same functions and properties as the category above it in the hierarchy. For example, the Node class contains a function called moveBy(x, y) that moves the node by an amount equal to whatever is passed as the arguments for the x and y axes. Because this function is part of the Node class, an Entity, Label, Sprite, Map, Group, or Scene can all call moveBy(). This is called inheritance.

Seeing Elements of a Game

When a game is created, not all parts of that game are immediately visible. If we create a shooting game where enemies appear at the top of the screen, not all the enemies will be visible at the beginning of the game. If they were, the game most likely would be either too difficult to beat or over very quickly.

Instead, we create and register enemies to a scene over time to make them visible. All the visible elements in a game are part of a hierarchy of objects called the *display object tree*. The root objects of the display object tree are called *scenes*. When a game is created, one scene is created by default. This default scene is known as the rootScene. Multiple scenes can be created, and multiple objects can be registered to the scenes in the display object tree, as shown in Figure 3-2.

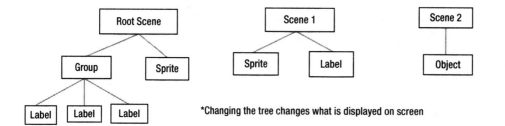

Figure 3-2. *Display object tree*

If the rootScene is the active scene, only the objects registered to it will be visible on the screen. Objects registered to Scene 1 or Scene 2 will not be visible. By adding objects to scenes, removing them, and changing which scene is the active one, we can change what appears on the screen during a game. We examine this with more hands-on detail through the code samples we provide later in the chapter.

Creating Labels

There are many occasions in a game when text needs to be displayed onscreen, such as when a user has a score that changes during play, a time limit is imposed on levels, or a main character has a specific amount of health. Any text that appears in a game, with the exception of stylized art, should reside in a label. Labels in enchant.js are created in a way that allows them to be easily manipulated in terms of font, color, and position.

As an initial exercise for this section, we walk through all the steps necessary to create an enchant.js game that creates labels of random position and color.

Setting Up a Game

When you write JavaScript that creates and executes a game, you must follow a specific format that initializes, or activates, the enchant.js library and specifies the game code to be run after the page loads. Follow these steps to see how:

1. Go to `http://code.9leap.net/codes/show/27204` and fork the code to have a workable blank template. You might need to log in or create an account to do this.

■ **Note** If you are not using code.9leap.net, you will need to import the enchant.js library into your project, which is covered in Chapter 1.

---

2. Type in the code shown in Listing 3-1.

    Listing 3-1. Initializing the enchant.js Library

    ```
    enchant();
    ```

This command tells enchant.js to initialize all the code necessary to create and run games.

3. Under that, type in the code shown in Listing 3-2.

    Listing 3-2. Creating window.onload()

    ```
    window.onload = function() {
    }
    ```

This instructs the browser to run the code in the curly brackets ({}) only after everything else has loaded. This ensures that everything necessary for enchant.js to run is present before the game actually starts. Every enchant.js game must have these two components to run. We enter almost all the code for a game inside the curly brackets.

Making the Core Object and Starting the Game

Now that we've completed the necessary groundwork for our game, we can create the core of the game, the Core object. The Core object is the game itself, and defines the size of the game when it is created. All elements of a game (scenes, labels, sprites, and so on) are created in this Core object. To create it, do the following:

1. Modify your `window.onload` statement to match Listing 3-3. This creates the Core object, specifying the size of the game to be 320 pixels wide (first argument) by 320 pixels tall (second argument). Assume that all code instructions past this point should be entered within the curly brackets, beneath the last line of code entered unless stated otherwise.

Listing 3-3. Creating the Core Object

```
window.onload = function() {
        var game = new Core(320, 320);
}
```

■ **Note**   Prior to version 0.6, the Core object was called the Game object. You might see notation using a Game object instead of a Core object (var game = new Game(320,320)) if you work with games created with earlier versions of enchant.js. This was changed because of the increasing use of enchant.js for non-game applications.

For all intents and purposes, if you encounter a Game object, you can treat it as a Core object.

---

2. Place your cursor at the end of the line that reads var game = new Core(320, 320); and press Enter a few times to move your cursor down a few lines. Type in the code in Listing 3-4. This command tells the game to start and should always appear at the end of your window.onload statement.

Listing 3-4. Starting the Game

```
game.start();
```

Creating a Label

The next step is to create a label with a message. Do the following to create one:

1. After the line var game = new Core(320, 320);, type in the code in Listing 3-5. This creates a label with the text we designate in quotes.

Listing 3-5. Creating a Label

```
var label = new Label("Hello World!");
```

Adding the Label to the rootScene

If you click the Run button at this point, nothing will happen. As we mentioned earlier, objects within a game must be added to an active scene to become visible. Do the following to add it:

1. Type in the code in Listing 3-6 below the last line of code entered. This adds the label we created to the rootScene.

Listing 3-6. Adding the Label to the rootScene

```
game.rootScene.addChild(label);
```

2. Click the Run button. "Hello World!" appears in the upper-left corner of the screen because the label is now part of the default scene, rootScene.

Changing a Label's Properties

We discussed earlier how objects in enchant.js have their own properties, which control characteristics about those objects in a game. To change the characteristics of a label, do the following:

1. Above the line game.rootScene.addChild(label);, type in the code in Listing 3-7. This makes several changes to the appearance of the label.

    Listing 3-7. Changing Properties of a Label

    ```
    label.font = "16px sans-serif";
    label.color = "rgb(255,0,0)";
    label.x = 50;
    label.y = 100;
    ```

2. Click Run. The label appears in a different location, font, and color.

Formatting Font

In Listing 3-7, we changed the font of the label with label.font = "16px sans-serif".

The first attribute specified is the size of the font. This is represented by a number, specifying the size of the font in pixels, and is followed by the letters "px" without a space between the two.

Next, the font's name is specified. It is possible to use predefined font names (font family names) such as "MS PGothic," but some devices do not contain these fonts. If a device without the specific font tries to render the label, the user might encounter an error. Errors are never fun for the user, which is why it is best to use general names for your fonts as shown below. Note that serifs are stylized points at the ends of letters, most commonly seen on letters used in print.

- *sans-serif:* Gothic-style typeface (without serifs)

- *serif:* Roman-style typeface (with serifs)

- *monospace:* Fixed-width font

Formatting Color

In Listing 3-7, we changed the color of the label with label.color = "rgb(255,0,0)";.

Color in enchant.js can be set for labels, and for any other element that accepts color, using any format valid for color in CSS (Cascading Style Sheets). Do not worry if you are not familiar with CSS, as we will cover the different formats here. There are six valid ways of assigning color in CSS, as shown in Table 3-1. As the property is defined as a string, make sure to enclose the assigned value within double quotation marks ("").

Table 3-1. *Different Ways to Specify the Color Red*

Value (red in this example)	Description
"#ff0000"	"#RRGGBB" format. The values are defined between "00~FF" as numbers in base 16.
"#f00"	"#RGB" format. The values are defined between "0~F" as numbers in base 16. This format creates the same color as "#ff0000" and is just an abbreviated format.
"rgb(255, 0, 0)"	"rgb(R, G, B)" format. The values are defined between "0~255" as numbers in base 10.
"rgb(100%, 0%, 0%)"	"rgb(R, G, B)" format. The values are defined between "0%~100%" as percentages in base 10.
"rgba(255,0,0,1.0)"	"rgba(R, G, B, A)" format. RGB is defined between "0~255" and the transmittance (alpha transparency) is defined between "0.0~1.0" (0 as fully transparent and 1 as fully opaque).
"red"	The color is defined by the name.

Also, most of the listings in Table 3-1 express a mixture of three colors: red, green, and blue. To specify red, we select the maximum value of red (ff in base 16) and the minimum value of green and blue (00 in base 16). In base 16, 0-9 are the same as base 10 (normal counting), then 10 = A, 11 = B, and so on, up to 16 = F. There is no difference between uppercase and lowercase letters in base 16 (also known as hexadecimal format).

Defining Position

Position is defined by setting values to the x and y properties of the label. In Listing 3-7, we set the position of the label to be 50 pixels from the left edge of the game screen with label.x = 50; and 100 pixels from the top edge of the game screen with label.y = 100;.

Creating a Function to Create Labels for Us

Optimization is a common concept in programming. It means using as little code as possible, or using code shortcuts, to create a game or other application. In our game we are going to create multiple labels, so it will be much easier for us to create a single function that creates and configures a label for us and can be called an infinite number of times than to manually create a label many times over. Do the following to see how:

1. Delete the code you wrote from Listings 3-6 and 3-7 and replace it with the code in Listing 3-8. This function will accept four arguments, create a Label with the text argument, specify the color to be whatever was indicated for the color argument, set the position with the x and y arguments, and then add the label to the rootScene.

Listing 3-8. Creating the addLabel Function

```
game.addLabel = function(text, color, x, y) {
        var label = new Label(text);
        label.font = "16px sans-serif";
        label.color = color;
        label.x = x;
        label.y = y;
        game.rootScene.addChild(label);
};
```

This does not by itself create a label. Rather, it contains instructions for creating a label. To create a label, we must call the function and provide the arguments.

2. Under the preceding code, type in the code in Listing 3-9.

Listing 3-9. Calling addLabel

```
game.addLabel("50 Points", "rgb(255,0,0)", 50, 50);
game.addLabel("100 Points", "rgb(50,0,100)", 50, 200);
```

3. Click Run. A red label and purple label will appear.

Creating a Random Number Function

Why do we need random numbers? Because we're going to assign random attributes to the labels we create, and need random numbers to do so. Do the following to create a random number function:

1. Go to the very bottom of your code, below the last semicolon of the `window.onload` statement, and type in the code in Listing 3-10.

Listing 3-10. Random Number Function

```
function rand(num){
        return Math.floor(Math.random() * num);
}
```

Both `floor()` and `random()` are methods of the `Math` object, a predefined object in JavaScript. This definition for the `rand()` function accepts one argument, `num`, that is multiplied by the result of `Math.random()`. `Math.random()` will return a decimal value between 0 and 1. `Math.floor` will round the result down to the closest whole number, and then the number will be returned (provided) as the result of the `rand()` function.

■ **Note** The range of decimal values `Math.random()` can return includes 0 but does not include 1. For example, if we were to multiply `Math.random()` by 100, the smallest value that could theoretically be returned is 0, and the largest value that could theoretically be returned is one very close to 100, but not quite 100 (in other words, something close to 99.99999999999). Rounding this down with `Math.floor()` gives us a possible random integer (whole number) value between 0 and 99.

For example, if we call `rand(100)` and the program returns 0.88134 as the returned value for `Math.random()`, it would first be multiplied by the argument we specified (100), becoming 88.134. Then it would be rounded down by `Math.floor()` to 88 and returned. The reasoning for creating this function will become evident in the next section.

Automating Label Creation with the ENTER_FRAME Event Listener and Periodic Processing

Now that we have the function necessary to create labels easily, we need something that can call the function at a fixed interval, also known as *periodic processing*. We can do this with an event listener. Event listeners are parts of code that are constantly on the lookout for a specific event, and when that event occurs the event listener triggers specific code that we create. Do the following to see how:

1. Delete the two game.addLabel() statements you created in Listing 3-9 and replace them with the code in Listing 3-11. This code instructs the program to execute the code within the curly braces ({}) every time the ENTER_FRAME event occurs. This event occurs every frame.

Listing 3-11. ENTER_FRAME Event Listener

```
game.rootScene.addEventListener(Event.ENTER_FRAME, function() {
});
```

You can create event listeners for any Node object (not just the rootScene), and set them to listen for any event in enchant.js. Table 3-2 lists the main events in enchant.js.

Table 3-2. *Events*

Event Type	Description	Event Issued By
Event.A_BUTTON_DOWN	Event occurring when the a button is pressed	core, scene
EventA_BUTTON_UP	Event occurring when the a button is released	core, scene
Event.ADDED	Event occurring when a node is added to a group	node
Event.ADDED_TO_SCENE	Event occurring when a node is added to a scene	node
Event.B_BUTTON_DOWN	Event occurring when the b button is pressed	core, scene
Event.B_BUTTON_UP	Event occurring when the b button is released	core, scene
Event.DOWN_BUTTON_DOWN	Event occurring when the down button is pressed	core, scene
Event.DOWN_BUTTON_UP	Event occurring when the down button is released	core, scene
Event.ENTER	Event occurring when a scene begins	scene
Event.ENTER_FRAME	Event occurring when a new frame is being processed	core, scene
Event.EXIT	Event occurring when the scene ends	scene
Event.EXIT_FRAME	Event occurring when frame processing is about to end	core
Event.INPUT_CHANGE	Event occurring when a button input changes	core, scene
Event.INPUT_END	Event occurring when a button input ends	core, scene
Event.INPUT_START	Event occurring when a button input begins	core, scene
Event.LEFT_BUTTON_DOWN	Event occurring when the left button is pressed	core, scene
Event.LEFT_BUTTON_UP	Event occurring when the left button is released	core, scene
Event.LOAD	Event dispatched upon completion of game loading	core
Event.PROGRESS	Events occurring during game loading	core

(continued)

Table 3-2. (*continued*)

Event Type	Description	Event Issued By
Event.REMOVED	Event occurring when a node is removed from a group	node
Event.REMOVED_FROM_SCENE	Event occurring when a node is removed from a scene	node
Event.RENDER	Event occurring when an entity is rendered	entity
Event.RIGHT_BUTTON_DOWN	Event occurring when the right button is pressed	core, scene
Event.RIGHT_BUTTON_UP	Event occurring when the right button is released	core, scene
Event.TOUCH_END	Event occurring when a touch related to the node has ended	node
Event.TOUCH_MOVE	Event occurring when a touch related to the node has moved	node
Event.TOUCH_START	Event occurring when a touch related to the node has begun	node
Event.UP_BUTTON_DOWN	Event occurring when the Up button is pressed	core, scene
Event.UP_BUTTON_UP	Event occurring when the Up button is released	core, scene

2. Type in the code in Listing 3-12 inside the curly braces to create and assign variables to represent a random score to be displayed; the value of red (in the RGB color component of the label), green, and blue; and the x and y position.

Listing 3-12. Creating Variables and Assigning Random Values

```
var score = rand(100);
var r = rand(256);
var g = rand(256);
var b = rand(256);
var x = rand(300);
var y = rand(300);
```

3. Below the code you just entered, but still inside the curly braces, call the addLabel() function we created earlier, passing the random variables as the arguments of the function, by typing in the code in Listing 3-13.

Listing 3-13. Calling the addLabel() Function

```
game.addLabel(score + " Points", "rgb(" + r + "," + g + "," + b + ")", x, y);
```

4. Click Run. Labels are created rapidly onscreen.

Slowing Down Processing with Frame and Modulo

Label creation might seem a bit out of control at this point because after you the click the Run button, it is not long before the entire screen becomes completely full of labels. Luckily, you can slow this down. Do the following to see how:

1. Enter the code you wrote in Listing 3-12 and 3-13 inside an if statement, as shown in Listing 3-14. Here, game.frame is equal to the number of frames that have elapsed in a game, and the modulo operator (%) will return the remainder after dividing the number of frames by 3. If that value is equal to 0, a label will be created. The final effect of this code is to cause a label to be created every third frame.

Listing 3-14. Controlling the Frequency of Label Creation

```
if (game.frame % 3 === 0) {
        var score = rand(100);
        var r = rand(256);
        var g = rand(256);
        var b = rand(256);
        var x = rand(300);
        var y = rand(300);
        game.addLabel(score + " Points", "rgb(" + r + "," + g + "," + b + ")", x, y);
}
```

2. Click Run. The labels are created at a much slower rate.

Removing Labels After a Specified Time

The labels are created more slowly now, but they still fill up the screen after a short amount of time. To clear a label after it is created, we need to use another event listener.

1. Type in the code in Listing 3-15 under game.rootScene.addChild(label); (still inside the window.onload function curly braces). Here, we add an event listener to the labels we create, specifying to remove the label from the document object tree if the label's age, or the number of frames the label has been part of the document object tree, exceeds 10 frames.

Listing 3-15. Removing the Label

```
label.addEventListener(Event.ENTER_FRAME, function() {
        if (label.age > 10) game.rootScene.removeChild(label);
});
```

Did you notice there are no curly braces after the if statement? This is because there is only one statement. Without curly braces, the if statement triggers only the subsequent single line of code.

2. Click Run. Labels are created randomly and then removed from the screen shortly after they are created.

Making Labels Move

As a final effect for our labels, we want them to move up after they are created. Do the following to instruct them to move up by one pixel every frame:

1. Directly above the if statement you entered from Listing 3-15, but still within the event listener curly braces, enter the code from Listing 3-16. This simply reduces the y position of the label by one.

Listing 3-16. Moving the Label

```
label.y --;
```

2. Because the ENTER_FRAME event listener executes its code every frame, the label moves up the screen at a rate of 30 frames every second, as the frames per second (fps) setting of the Core object is set to 30 fps by default.

■ **Note**   You can change the frames per second setting by modifying the `fps` property of the Core object (in other words, game.fps = 16;).

---

3. Click Run. The labels are displayed and will move up the screen before disappearing.

Labels are used for showing scores and more in games, and the preceding exercise gave you a brief look at how to create them. We will use them much more as we continue. If you encounter any problems, you can find a fully working code sample at http://code.9leap.net/codes/show/27211.

Creating Sprites

Although there are exceptions, most games have a main character, or enemies, or allies, or characters of some kind. These characters are represented by images and usually move around in some capacity. In enchant.js, characters are represented by sprites. When a sprite is created, it comes equipped with a number of properties and methods that make it easier to manipulate.

Setting Up a Game for Sprites

To set up your game for sprites, you need to preload images for the sprites and create a game.onload statement. Do the following to see how to create a bear sprite that walks across the screen:

1. Fork the blank enchant.js template from http://code.9leap.net/codes/show/27204.

2. Type in the code in Listing 3-17 to create the basic structure of the game. Here, we use the preload function to load in the image of a bear to be used for the sprite. This image is included in the project on code.9leap.net and was included when you forked it in the preceding step.

Listing 3-17. Basic Structure of the Bear Game

```
enchant();
        window.onload = function() {
        var game = new Core(320, 320);
        game.preload('chara1.gif');

        game.onload = function() {

        };

        game.start();
    };
```

This code sample also includes the game.onload function that is necessary when loading in images or doing more than just adding and removing nodes and event listeners. This function, similar to window.onload, executes its code after the game has fully been loaded.

Creating a Sprite

To create a sprite, a variable to represent the sprite must be declared, an image must be assigned to it, and then it must be added to the document object tree. The following steps show you how to complete this process:

1. Create a variable to represent a 32-pixel-wide by 32-pixel-tall sprite by typing in the code in Listing 3-18 inside the game.onload function. You can assume that all future references to placing code inside a function mean to place that code inside the curly braces at the end of that function.

    Listing 3-18. Creating the Sprite Variable

    ```
    var bear = new Sprite(32, 32);
    ```

2. Assign the image you preloaded in the last section by typing in the code in Listing 3-19 on the next line.

    Listing 3-19. Assigning an Image to the Image Property

    ```
    bear.image = game.assets['chara1.gif'];
    ```

3. On the next line, add the bear to the rootScene to make it visible by typing in the code in Listing 3-20.

    Listing 3-20. Making the Bear Visible

    ```
    game.rootScene.addChild(bear);
    ```

4. Click Run. The bear appears in the upper-left corner of the screen.

Specifying the Frame of a Sprite

If you are using code.9leap.net for this project, you will see chara1.gif represented on the right side of the screen by a thumbnail image. This image contains several pictures of bears, so why does only one bear appear in our game currently? The answer has to do with frames.

When you create a sprite with Sprite(32,32), the program creates the sprite with the dimensions of 32 pixels by 32 pixels. When you assign an image to the sprite, the program slices that image into frames of the same size and identifies them by number, starting with 0. This concept, called the *frame index*, is shown as it applies to chara1.gif in Figure 3-3.

Figure 3-3. *Frame Index*

You can select the frame for a sprite by setting the desired frame number as the frame property. To do so with our bear, do the following:

5. Select the white standing bear as the frame by inserting the code in Listing 3-21 above the game.rootScene.addChild(bear); statement. Inserting the code after the addChild function carries the risk of the brown bear appearing onscreen and then switching to the image of the white bear.

Listing 3-21. Assigning the White Bear Frame

```
bear.frame = 5;
```

6. Click Run. The sprite appears as a white bear.

Animating a Sprite

It's great that we have an image, but the real point of a frame is to create the illusion of movement. Eventually, we will instruct the bear to move back and forth across the screen because we want the bear to appear as though it is walking. In our chara1.gif image, there are a few images of the white bear that we can show in rapid succession to achieve this. Do the following to see how:

1. Replace the bear.frame line you just added with the code shown in Listing 3-22. This notation is an array of numbers and acts as a shortcut for animation. For each frame, the frame will move to the next indicated frame in the sequence.

Listing 3-22. Animating the Bear

```
bear.frame = [5, 6, 5, 7];
```

2. Click Run. The bear sprite rapidly cycles through the frames. This was the goal, but as it is now the bear seems a little neurotic. Let's slow him down a bit.

3. Rewrite your bear.frame statement to match the code in Listing 3-23. This slows down the rate of the frame change by assigning the same image for two frames instead of just one.

Listing 3-23. Slowing Down the Bear Frames

```
bear.frame = [5,5,6,6,5,5,7,7];
```

▪ **Note** Instead of using Listing 3-23, you could slow down how fast the bear changes frames by writing a `game.fps = 16;` statement before the game starts to make the game process 16 frames per second instead of the default 30. Keep in mind that this will slow down the frame rate for all entities inside the game.

---

4. Click Run. The bear changes frames at a more normal rate for walking.

Moving a Sprite

The sprite now has the appropriate animation for walking, but doesn't move. Do the following to move the bear across the screen:

1. Create an event listener on the bear sprite registered to the ENTER_FRAME event by typing in the code in Listing 3-24 under `game.rootScene.addChild(bear);`. Enter the code inside the curly braces of the `game.onload` function.

   Listing 3-24. Creating an Event Listener on the Bear

   ```
   bear.addEventListener(Event.ENTER_FRAME, function() {
   });
   ```

2. Create periodic processing inside the event listener to move the bear to the right by increasing the x position by 3, as shown in Listing 3-25.

   Listing 3-25. Moving the Bear

   ```
   bear.x += 3;
   ```

3. Click Run. The bear runs across and off the screen.

4. Create an `if` statement to move the bear only to the right if the bear's location is less than the edge of the screen by modifying Listing 3-25 to match Listing 3-26. We use 320 – 32 because, while 320 is the edge of the right side of the game screen, the position of the sprite is measured from the top-left corner. When the sprite is at x = 320, the bear will not be visible. Since 32 is the width of the sprite, putting the limit of the bear at 320 – 32 ensures the bear stays onscreen.

   Listing 3-26. Constraining Movement with an If Statement

   ```
   if (bear.x < 320 - 32) bear.x += 3;
   ```

Orienting a Sprite to Match Its Movement

Let's make the bear sprite walk back and forth across the screen facing whichever direction it is walking. To do this, we use the scaleX property. Do the following to see how:

1. Insert the code in Listing 3-27 above the game.rootScene.addChild(bear); statement. The scaleX property defaults to the value of 1 when the sprite is created and can be modified to change the size of the bear (in other words, scaleX = 2; will scale the bear to 200%). By making scaleX a negative value, the image of the bear is flipped across the x-axis, making the bear face the left side of the screen.

Listing 3-27. Inverting the Bear across the X Axis

```
bear.scaleX = -1;
```

■ **Note** A sprite image can be inverted across the y axis using sprite.scaleY = -1;.

---

2. Click Run. The bear appears to walk backward across the screen. This isn't what we're looking for as an end result, but it gives you an idea of how the scaleX property works. We'll use the scaleX property to dictate how the bear moves in the next few steps.

3. Delete the code you entered in Listing 3-26.

4. Replace the if statement (if (bear.x < 320 - 32) bear.x += 3;) in the bear's event listener with Listing 3-28. This code sample specifies that if the bear is facing right, it should move to the right by 3 pixels for each frame and should be flipped to face left if the bear reaches the right side of the screen. If the bear faces left, the bear should move to the left by 3 pixels for each frame and should be turned around to face right again when it reaches the left side of the screen.

Listing 3-28. Orienting the Bear

```
if (bear.scaleX === 1) {
        bear.x += 3;
        if (bear.x > 320 - 32) bear.scaleX = -1;
} else {
        bear.x -= 3;
        if (bear.x < 0) bear.scaleX = 1;
}
```

5. Click Run. The bear moves as described.

By now you should be getting familiar with the use of event listeners to process code on every frame. This is the core of many games in enchant.js. If you encounter any problems with the Sprite code, you can find a fully working code sample at http://code.9leap.net/codes/show/27365.

Drawing a Map with a Surface

Maps in enchant.js are made up of several small images called *tiles*. Imagine you are creating a game with tiles of green grass in the background and a character who moves around on the screen. To create a map filled with green grass tiles in enchant.js, you need to first add those tiles to a Surface object.

A Surface object is an object in enchant.js used for drawing. Drawing refers to the act of creating shapes (which will not be covered here) or images on an object. Once the surface is drawn on, it is then assigned as the image property of a sprite to join it to the display object tree. Using a Surface object allows multiple images to be drawn on a single object, which makes it a prime candidate for displaying a map. In the following code sample, we create a map comprised entirely of green grass tiles.

Setting up the Game

Do the following to set up an example game to use a Surface object:

1. Fork the blank enchant.js template from http://code.9leap.net/codes/show/27204.

2. Set the groundwork for your game by typing in the code in Listing 3-29. The preloaded map0.gif file, shown in Figure 3-4, contains the component tile images that we will use to create the map.

Listing 3-29. Setting up the Game

```
enchant();
window.onload = function() {
        var game = new Core(320, 320);
        game.fps = 16;

        game.preload('http://enchantjs.com/assets/images/map0.gif');

        game.start();
};
```

Figure 3-4. map0.gif

Creating Containers for a Map

A map must have a few containers to work with before we can populate it with tiles. Do the following to create them:

1. Below the preload statement, type in the code in Listing 3-30. Here, we create a variable to act as the sprite, which will display the map. We assign our preloaded map image to the variable maptip, which makes it easier to reference later. Finally, we create a new Surface, which is what we will draw our map tiles on.

Listing 3-30. Creating Containers

```
game.onload = function() {
        var bg = new Sprite(320, 320);
        var maptip = game.assets['http://enchantjs.com/assets/images/map0.gif'];
        var image = new Surface(320, 320);
};
```

Populating the Map with Tiles

A Surface object is drawn on with the `draw()` command. For our purposes in this section, think of the `draw()` command as used to copy and paste images onto a surface. Since our 16x16 tile images must be pasted one at a time onto our blank surface, we could write a very long list of these statements to draw the tiles, but doing this with a loop saves us time. Do the following to create the loop:

1.   Create two for loops to represent x and y coordinates by typing in the code in Listing 3-31 below `var image = new Surface(320,320);` but still inside the `game.onload` function.

   Listing 3-31. Tile Loops

```
for (var j = 0; j < 320; j += 16) {
        for (var i = 0; i < 320; i += 16) {


        }
}
```

This may appear confusing at first, but putting together two `for` loops is an incredibly useful tool for moving around on a Surface incrementally, which is exactly what we need to do to place tiles at specific intervals on the map.

Think of the variables j and i as y and x coordinates, respectively, for an imaginary cursor on a blank background. Imagine this blank background is cut into 16-pixel by 16-pixel squares, making a giant table. Variable j represents the row position of our imaginary cursor, and variable i represents the column position. This imaginary cursor is always pointed at the top-left corner of one of the 16 x 16 squares because that is the starting point for all operations that use the `draw()` function.

When the first `for` loop is entered, j has a value of 0. The second `for` loop is then entered, where i also has a starting value of 0. Our imaginary cursor is currently at (0,0), in the upper-left corner of the table. We will use this position in a `draw()` command to copy a tile, which isn't shown yet. After the `draw()` command, the second `for` loop repeats, this time with an i value of 16. Our `draw()` command will now run at (16,0). This repeats until i becomes 320. At this time, the first row of tiles will be filled with green tiles. Then, the first `for` loop repeats and the process starts over with the second row, and so on.

But let's not get ahead of ourselves. We have to actually create the `draw()` command first for this to work.

2.   Inside the second `for` loop, create the `draw()` command to actually copy the tiles throughout the for loop by copying Listing 3-32 into the second for loop (`for (var i = 0; i < 320; i += 16) {}`).

   Listing 3-32. The Draw Command to Copy Tiles

```
image.draw(maptip, 0, 0, 16, 16, i, j, 16, 16);
```

Yes, this command has a lot of arguments. Here's what they do:

- `maptip`: This is the preloaded image asset to be used as the source image (image of the tiles to be used on the map).

- `0, 0`: These are x and y coordinates of the upper-left corner of an imaginary rectangle that will be used to capture an area from the original image. If you were to imagine clicking and dragging a selection box over an image to copy a section of it, this would be the starting point of the click.

- `16, 16`: These are x and y coordinates of the lower-right corner of the imaginary rectangle to capture an area from the source image. If you were clicking and dragging to create a selection box, these would be the coordinates of where you let go of the click.

- **i, j:** These are the x and y coordinates on the destination Surface, which indicate the upper-left corner of where the captured image will be pasted. Going through the for loop changes these values to perfectly space the tiles over the course of the several draw() statements called.

- **16, 16:** The last two values indicate the width and height of the image to be pasted. If these are changed from the size of the captured area, it will scale the image before pasting it.

Assigning the Map to the Background and Displaying It

Now that we have copied tiles onto the destination Surface, we need to add it to the bg sprite so we can add it to the display object tree.

1. Under the for loops, but still inside the game.onload function, type in the code in Listing 3-33.

   Listing 3-33. Adding the Map

   ```
   bg.image = image;
   game.rootScene.addChild(bg);
   ```

2. Click Run. The map appears, filled with green grass tiles.

Maps form the background of many games in enchant.js. Although the techniques for creating them can be complicated to learn, familiarizing yourself with them will prove invaluable for creating more immersive games.

Using Touch to Interact

The next step for creating a game with a moving player on a grassy landscape is to create a character who, when the player clicks the screen, moves to that spot on the screen. This is accomplished with touch events, which occur when the user clicks on the game screen.

Creating a Character

It is important to remember that games in enchant.js are controlled primarily by loops that are run every frame. If we have a character that walks around the screen, it will have to have sets of sprites for each direction of movement, and be processed accordingly. Do the following to see how this is done:

1. At the very top of your code, before the enchant() command, add constants (values that will not change) by typing in the code in Listing 3-34. These values are used for specifying sprites for movement.

   Listing 3-34. Creating Directional Constants

   ```
   var DIR_LEFT  = 0;
   var DIR_RIGHT = 1;
   var DIR_UP    = 2;
   var DIR_DOWN  = 3;
   ```

2. Add chara0.gif (Figure 3-5) to the list of images to be preloaded by modifying the game.preload statement to the one shown in Listing 3-35.

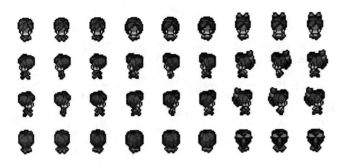

Figure 3-5. *chara0.gif*

Listing 3-35. Adding chara0.gif to the Images to be Loaded

```
game.preload('http://enchantjs.com/assets/images/chara0.gif',
        'http://enchantjs.com/assets/images/map0.gif');
```

3. Create a variable to represent our character, the girl from chara0.gif, and set the basic properties of that character by typing in the code in Listing 3-36 directly under game.rootScene.addChild(bg);. Setting the x and y coordinates to 160 – 16 causes the character to appear directly in the center of the screen. The frame is set to 7 to show the girl facing down first.

Listing 3-36. Creating the Basic Girl Character

```
var girl = new Sprite(32, 32);
girl.image = game.assets['http://enchantjs.com/assets/images/chara0.gif'];
girl.x     = 160 - 16;
girl.y     = 160 - 16;
girl.frame = 7;
```

4. Create secondary properties for the girl and add her to the document object tree by typing in the code in Listing 3-37 directly below the preceding code. The toX and toY properties are created to represent the location the girl will head toward when a player clicks the screen. The girl.anim array represents frame numbers used for animating the walking motion of the girl for all four directions.

Listing 3-37. Creating Secondary Properties for the Girl

```
girl.toX    = girl.x;
girl.toY    = girl.y;
girl.dir    = DIR_DOWN;
girl.anim   = [
        15, 16, 17, 16, //Left
        24, 25, 26, 24, //Right
        33, 34, 35, 34, //Up
         6,  7,  8,  7]; //Down
game.rootScene.addChild(girl);
```

5. Click Run. The girl appears on the screen in front of the grass tiles.

Processing Movement from Touch

The last step is to set up an event listener to move the girl if toX and toY are substantially different from the girl's current position and to process touch events made by the user. Do the following to see how:

1. Create an event listener for the girl character to process movement by typing in the code in Listing 3-38 under game.rootScene.addChild(girl);. Like all ENTER_FRAME event listeners, this will be processed on the girl sprite for every frame.

    Listing 3-38. Creating the Event Listener for the Girl

    ```
    girl.addEventListener(Event.ENTER_FRAME, function() {
    };
    ```

2. Within the event listener you just added, create an if statement to process the upward movement of the girl by typing in the code in Listing 3-39. This code sample states that if the current Y position of the girl is lower (greater) than the girl's destination (toY), the girl's direction should be set as DIR_UP and the girl should be moved up by 3 pixels each frame, unless the girl's current Y position is within 3 pixels of the destination. This is done by checking to see if the absolute value (Math.abs()) of the girl's Y position minus the girl's destination Y position is less than 3 pixels.

    Listing 3-39. Processing Upward Movement

    ```
    if (girl.y > girl.toY) {
            girl.dir = DIR_UP;
            if (Math.abs(girl.y - girl.toY) < 3) {
                    girl.y=girl.toY;
            } else {
                    girl.y -= 3;
            }
    }
    ```

3. Add the code to process the movement for the remaining directions (down, left, and right) by typing in the code in Listing 3-40 under the code you just added, but still within the girl's event listener. This code uses the exact same approach as the preceding code to move the girl in the appropriate direction.

    Listing 3-40. Processing the Other Directions of Movement

    ```
    else if (girl.y < girl.toY) {
            girl.dir = DIR_DOWN;
            if (Math.abs(girl.y - girl.toY) < 3) {
                    girl.y = girl.toY;
            } else {
                    girl.y += 3;
            }
    }
    ```

```
if (girl.x > girl.toX) {
        girl.dir = DIR_LEFT;
        if (Math.abs(girl.x - girl.toX) < 3) {
                girl.x = girl.toX;
        } else {
                girl.x -= 3;
        }
}

else if (girl.x < girl.toX) {
        girl.dir = DIR_RIGHT;
        if (Math.abs(girl.x- girl.toX) < 3) {
                girl.x = girl.toX;
        } else {
                girl.x += 3;
        }
}
```

4. Specify how the girl should be animated by adding Listing 3-41 directly under the last code you entered, still inside the girl's event listener. This code sample states that if the girl is not moving, her age should be made to equal 1. Every frame, the girl's age will increase; however, if she is standing still, her age will be reset to 1. This is used in the frame assignment on the next line to keep the girl from being animated if she is not moving. In the next line, the frame is assigned as a number from the array of values we specified earlier. The code means that the frame of the girl should cycle through the four frames of a given direction the girl is traveling in or facing.

Listing 3-41. Animating the Girl

```
if (girl.x == girl.toX && girl.y == girl.toY) girl.age = 1;
girl.frame = girl.anim[girl.dir * 4 + (girl.age % 4)];
```

5. Create the TOUCH_START and TOUCH_MOVE event listeners to capture clicks from the player and save those values to the girl's toX and toY properties by modifying the last part of your code to match Listing 3-42. The two event listeners should be added inside the game.onload function, but outside the girl's ENTER_FRAME event listener. Here, the TOUCH events are being passed into the functions as an argument (function(e)) and include the X and Y coordinates of where the touch event happens. Assigning those coordinates to the girl's toX and toY properties (with -16 to center the girl) move the girl to the location being touched by the player.

Listing 3-42. Including Event Listeners for Touch

```
              ...if (girl.x == girl.toX && girl.y == girl.toY) girl.age = 1;
              girl.frame = girl.anim[girl.dir * 4 + (girl.age % 4)];

});

bg.addEventListener(Event.TOUCH_START, function(e){
        girl.toX = e.x - 16;
        girl.toY = e.y - 16;
});
```

```
                    bg.addEventListener(Event.TOUCH_MOVE, function(e){
                            girl.toX = e.x - 16;
                            girl.toY = e.y - 16;
                    });
            };
        game.start();
    };
```

6. Click Run. The girl now follows mouse clicks on the screen, walking towards them.

This section introduced some complex tricks for controlling sprites with touch events. Enabling this ability for your sprites will create smoother and more enjoyable games for your players.

Using D-Pads to Interact

So far, the only interaction between player and game we have seen has been with touch events. However, this isn't the only way players can interact with games. To support interaction outside of touch events, enchant.js comes with a plug-in for putting both digital and analog directional pads (d-pads) into your games. Digital d-pads (Figure 3-6) involve only four directional buttons (up, down, left, right), while analog pads are control sticks manipulated by a user's thumb. The control sticks on Playstation 2 and 3 controllers are good examples of real-life analog pads. The analog pad passes X and Y values of the current location of the stick relative to its center. We do not cover analog pads in this book; instead, we focus on digital d-pads.

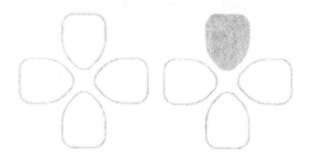

Figure 3-6. *Digital D-Pad*

In the code sample for this section, we create a digital d-pad that gives you the foundation for a sidescroller game, with a bear character and a floor. Pressing the d-pad moves the bear in the direction specified.

Creating a D-Pad

Do the following to create the d-pad:

1. Fork the code at http://code.9leap.net/codes/show/27476 to create the basis of the game. If you are not using code.9leap.net, copy the code from Listing 3-43 into a new code file.

Listing 3-43. Foundation of the D-Pad Game

```
var STATUS_WAIT = 0;
var STATUS_WALK = 1;
var STATUS_JUMP = 2;
```

```
enchant();
window.onload = function() {
    //create game object
    var game = new Core(320, 320);
    game.fps = 16;

    //load images
    game.preload('http://enchantjs.com/assets/images/chara1.gif',
        'http://enchantjs.com/assets/images/map0.gif');

    //called when the loading is complete
    game.onload = function() {
        //create the background
        var bg = new Sprite(320, 320);
        bg.backgroundColor = "rgb(0, 200, 255)";
        var maptip = game.assets['http://enchantjs.com/assets/images/map0.gif'];
        var image = new Surface(320, 320);
        for (var i = 0; i < 320; i += 16) {
            image.draw(maptip, 3 * 16, 0, 16, 16, i, 320 - 16, 16, 16);
        }
        bg.image = image;
        game.rootScene.addChild(bg);

        //The d-pad should be created below this line

        //create bear
        var bear = new Sprite(32, 32);
        bear.image  = game.assets['http://enchantjs.com/assets/images/chara1.gif'];
        bear.x      = 160 - 16;
        bear.y      = 320 - 16 - 32;
        bear.status = STATUS_WAIT;
        bear.anim   = [10, 11, 10, 12];
        bear.frame  = 10;
        game.rootScene.addChild(bear);

        //frame loop for the bear
        bear.addEventListener(Event.ENTER_FRAME, function() {

            //frame setting
            if (bear.status == STATUS_WAIT) {
                bear.frame = bear.anim[0];
            } else if (bear.status == STATUS_WALK) {
                bear.frame = bear.anim[bear.age % 4];
            } else if (bear.status == STATUS_JUMP) {
                bear.frame = bear.anim[1];
            }
        });
    };

    //start game
    game.start();
};
```

■ **Note** D-pads require loading of the ui.enchant.js plug-in. This is shown in the index.html file within the code.9leap example, and involves adding `<script src='/static/enchant.js-latest/plugins/ui.enchant.js'></script>` or a similar pointer to the file in the header of the index.html file that calls the enchant.js game script.

---

2. Create the D-pad by typing in the code in Listing 3-44 under the comment line that says `//The d-pad should be created below this line`. This creates the D-pad at (0,220).

Listing 3-44. Creating a D-Pad

```
var pad = new Pad();
pad.x   = 0;
pad.y   = 220;
game.rootScene.addChild(pad);
```

3. Click Run. The D-pad appears in the lower-left corner of the screen.

Processing Movement with the D-Pad

You've created the D-pad, but you still need to program it to move the bear. Do the following to make it happen:

1. Tie the D-pad in with the movement of the bear by adding Listing 3-45 to the inside of the Bear's ENTER_FRAME event listener (directly under `bear.addEventListener (Event.ENTER_FRAME, function() { }`. This ties in the input from the d-pad with commands to move the bear.

Listing 3-45. Processing Movement with the D-Pad

```
//up
if (bear.status != STATUS_JUMP) {
        bear.status = STATUS_WAIT;
        if (game.input.up)  {
                bear.status = STATUS_JUMP;
                bear.age = 0;
        }
}

//left
if (game.input.left)  {
        bear.x -= 3;
        bear.scaleX = -1;
        if (bear.status != STATUS_JUMP) bear.status = STATUS_WALK;
}

//right
else if (game.input.right) {
        bear.x += 3;
        bear.scaleX =  1;
        if (bear.status != STATUS_JUMP) bear.status = STATUS_WALK;
}
```

```
//when jumping
if (bear.status == STATUS_JUMP) {
        if (bear.age < 8) {
                bear.y -= 8;
        } else if (bear.age < 16) {
                bear.y += 8;
        } else {
                bear.status = STATUS_WAIT;
        }
}
```

2. Click Run. The D-Pad now controls the movement of the bear.

D-pads, like touch events, can be used to move characters and are a useful element if you do not want to use targeting by means of touch events. They are especially useful if you want to give your game a retro feel.

Conclusion

This concludes the chapter on the basics of enchant.js. We've used code samples to create labels, sprites, surfaces, touch events, and virtual pads. You now have a strong foundation for creating your own basic game in enchant.js. You might not use all the elements we examined when you create your own game, but there's a very high chance you will use at least some of them because most enchant.js games use labels and sprites.

In the next chapter, we cover some of the more advanced features of enchant.js, such as navigating between scenes, adding a start screen and game over screen, creating an advanced map, and establishing sound playback. These tools allow you to take your games to a higher level of complexity and creativity.

■ ■ ■

CHAPTER 4

Advanced Features of enchant.js

The basics of enchant.js allow simple game creation. More advanced features, such as navigation between scenes within a single game, require the use of more complex capabilities of enchant.js. In this chapter, we demonstrate how to create scene transitions for including multiple levels or environments, start and game over screens that polish your game's appearance, and maps and sounds to increase interactivity.

Summary List

1. Transitioning Between Scenes

2. Creating Start, Game Over, and Score Sharing Screens

3. Using Collision Detection

4. Creating an Interactive Map

Transitioning Between Scenes

While a single scene might be sufficient for simple games, any type of adventure or dialogue-based game needs multiple scenes to maintain a genre-appropriate feel.

The sample code for this section shows how to create a simple program that uses scene transitions to enable players to switch between three different scenes. Figure 4-1 illustrates how players can navigate between the three scenes by clicking on the orange navigational text.

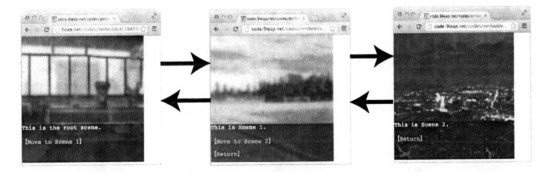

Figure 4-1. *Scene transitions*

Anatomy of a Scene

Scenes can be a challenging because they have their own structure that is different from other entities in enchant.js. Because of this, we provide you with some fundamental information in this section about how scenes work, followed by sample code to show how scenes are used in actual enchant.js games.

Scene Creation

A scene is a screen unit into which display objects like sprites, labels, maps and groups can be added. One game can have multiple scenes, and by switching scenes, you can completely change the content of the screen. Common types of scenes include the title screen, play screen, and game over screen. To create scenes, the Scene object constructor (var scene1 = new Scene();) is used.

Scene Stack

After you create a scene, you can add the background, labels with text, and sprites to the scene. Once that is complete, add the scene to the scene stack with the addChild() function.

Scenes are organized in a stack structure. As the term "stack" implies, multiple scenes are stacked on top of each other. The top-most scene is the visible scene. You add a scene to the top of the stack with the push() method, and you remove the top-most scene with the pop() method, as illustrated in Figure 4-2.

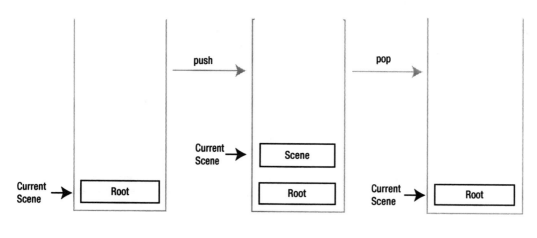

Stack Construction

Figure 4-2. *Stack construction*

Scene Properties and Methods

Inside a game, you can reference the current scene with currentScene and the root scene with rootScene. These two names make it easy to keep track of what is going on in your game's scene stack.

Table 4-1 shows the methods for Scene objects.

Table 4-1. *Scene Object Methods*

Code (Argument)	Description
pushScene(Scene)	Switches to a new scene, adding it to the top of the scene stack.
popScene()	Ends the current scene by removing it from the screen stack. The underlying scene, if there is one, becomes the new current scene.
removeScene(scene)	Removes the specified scene from the stack.
replaceScene(scene)	Replaces the current scene with another scene.

Carrying Out Scene Transitions

To create code that allows a player to transition between three scenes, do the following:

1. Fork the code from http://code.9leap.net/codes/show/27650. If you cannot access the code, copy it from Listing 4-1.

    Listing 4-1. Setting up for Scenes

```
enchant();
window.onload = function() {
    //Core object creation
    var game = new Core(320, 320);
    game.fps = 16;

    //Image loading
    game.preload('http://enchantjs.com/assets/images/bg/bg01.jpg',
        'http://enchantjs.com/assets/images/bg/bg02.jpg',
        'http://enchantjs.com/assets/images/bg/bg03.jpg');

    //Called when pre-loading is complete
    game.onload = function() {

        //Background creation
        var bg = makeBackground(game.assets
        ['http://enchantjs.com/assets/images/bg/bg01.jpg'])
        game.rootScene.addChild(bg);

        //Message creation
        game.rootScene.addChild(makeMessage("This is the root scene."));

        //Choice button creation
        var select=makeSelect("[Move to Scene 1]", 320 - 32 * 2);
        select.addEventListener(Event.TOUCH_START, function(e) {
            game.pushScene(game.makeScene1());
        });
        game.rootScene.addChild(select);
    };
```

```javascript
        //Scene 1 creation
    game.makeScene1 = function() {
        var scene = new Scene();

        //Background creation
        var bg = makeBackground(game.assets
        ['http://enchantjs.com/assets/images/bg/bg02.jpg'])
        scene.addChild(bg);

        //Message creation
        scene.addChild(makeMessage("This is Scene 1."));

        //Choice button creation
        var select = makeSelect("【Move to Scene 2】", 320 - 32 * 2);
        select.addEventListener(Event.TOUCH_START, function(e) {
            game.pushScene(game.makeScene2());
        });
        scene.addChild(select);
        scene.addChild(makeReturn(1));
        return scene;
    };

        //Scene 2 creation
    game.makeScene2 = function() {
        var scene = new Scene();

        //Background creation
        var bg = makeBackground(game.assets
        ['http://enchantjs.com/assets/images/bg/bg03.jpg'])
        scene.addChild(bg);

        //Label creation
        scene.addChild(makeMessage("This is Scene 2."));
        scene.addChild(makeReturn(0));
        return scene;
    };

    //Start game
    game.start();
};

//Background creation
function makeBackground(image) {
    var bg = new Sprite(320, 320);
    bg.image = image;
    return bg;
}
//Message creation
function makeMessage(text) {
    var label = new Label(text);
    label.font   = "16px monospace";
```

```
        label.color = "rgb(255,255,255)";
        label.backgroundColor = "rgba(0,0,0,0.6)";
        label.y      = 320 - 32 * 3;
        label.width = 320;
        label.height = 32 * 3;
        return label;
    }

    //Choice button creation
    function makeSelect(text, y) {
        var label = new Label(text);
        label.font  = "16px monospace";
        label.color = "rgb(255,200,0)";
        label.y      = y;
        label.width = 320;
        return label;
    }

    //Return button creation
    function makeReturn(lineNumber) {
        var game = enchant.Game.instance;
        var returnLabel = makeSelect("【Return】", 320 - 32 * (2-lineNumber));
        returnLabel.addEventListener(Event.TOUCH_START, function(e) {
            game.popScene();
        });
        return returnLabel;
    }
```

In this program, when a player clicks the Move to Scene 1 button, the game displays Scene 1. The method pushScene() should make sense, but what about game.pushScene(game.makeScene1());?

In the preceding sample code, we explicitly define the makeScene1() and makeScene2() methods for our Core object class. When the methods are called, they create and return a scene.

All that is happening in this function is the creation of a Scene object, followed by the creation and addition of various elements to that scene. First, the code creates a background and adds it to the scene. Next, the code creates and adds a label to the scene, specifically using the makeMessage() function we've created. The code then adds it to the scene with addChild(). After that, the code creates another label by the same means, which allows navigation to Scene 2.

The last line of the method returns the scene. Remember that adding elements to the scene does not actually make the scene active, which is why this return is here. Doing this allows us to put it inside the pushScene() function, which will call makeScene1() and then use the scene it creates, pushing it to the top of the stack.

When a player clicks the Return button from within either scene 1 or scene 2, the scene at the top of the scene stack is removed by means of popScene().

Scenes allow multiple environments to exist within the same game. You can use them for levels or images in a dialog-based game. However, you don't have to include them in your game. Many popular games in enchant.js are created without the specific use of scenes.

Creating a Game with Screens, Time Limits, and Scores

Start and game over screens are useful tools for communicating to your players the beginning and ending of a game. Luckily, enchant.js comes with an official plug-in, nineleap.enchant.js, for making these screens easy to implement.

In the sample code in this section, we create a game that begins with a start screen. When a player clicks the start screen, a transition to the root scene occurs. Within the root scene, the player can use a d-pad to control the left and right movement of a bear to catch apples falling from the top of the screen. Collecting apples increases the player's score. After a 10-second time limit is reached, the game stops and the game over screen is displayed. Figure 4-3 shows the sequence of screen transitions.

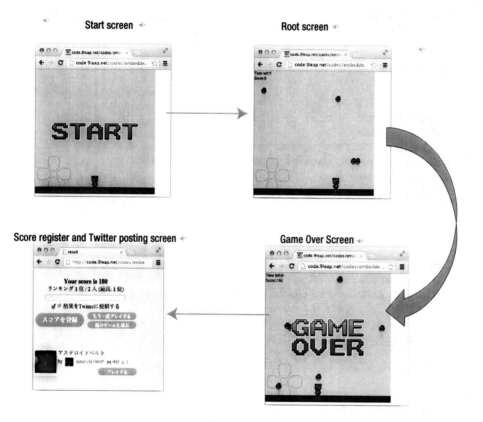

Figure 4-3. *Sequence of screens from the nineleap sample project code*

If you upload your game to 9leap.net, the game over screen will be followed by another screen that shows the player's score.

Setting Up a Sample Game

We first need a game to implement a start and end screen for. To create this game, do the following:

1. Fork the code from http://code.9leap.net/codes/show/23342 to your own project on code.9leap.net. If you are not using code.9leap.net, copy and paste the code from Listing 4-2. This code is for a simple apple-catching game.

Listing 4-2. Apple-Catching Game

```
enchant();
window.onload = function() {
    //Game object creation
    var game = new Core(320, 320);
    game.fps = 16;
    game.score = 0;
    var label;
    var bear;

    //Image loading
    game.preload('chara1.gif',
        'http://enchantjs.com/assets/images/map0.gif',
        'http://enchantjs.com/assets/images/icon0.gif');

    //Called when the loading is complete
    game.onload = function() {
        //Background creation
        var bg = new Sprite(320, 320);
        bg.backgroundColor = "rgb(0, 200, 255)";
        var maptip = game.assets['http://enchantjs.com/assets/images/map0.gif'];
        var image = new Surface(320, 320);
        for (var i = 0; i < 320; i += 16) {
            image.draw(maptip, 7 * 16, 0, 16, 16, i, 320 - 16, 16, 16);
        }
        bg.image = image;
        game.rootScene.addChild(bg);

        //Virtual pad creation
        var pad = new Pad();
        pad.x   = 0;
        pad.y   = 220;
        game.rootScene.addChild(pad);

        //Label creation
        label = new Label("");
        game.rootScene.addChild(label);

        //Bear creation
        bear = new Sprite(32, 32);
        bear.image  = game.assets['chara1.gif'];
        bear.x      = 160 - 16;
        bear.y      = 320 - 16 - 32;
```

```
        bear.anim    = [10, 11, 10, 12];
        bear.frame   = bear.anim[0];
        game.rootScene.addChild(bear);

        //Periodic processing of the bear sprite
        bear.addEventListener(Event.ENTER_FRAME, function() {
            //Left
            if (game.input.left)  {
                bear.x -= 3;
                bear.scaleX = -1;
            }
            //Right
            else if (game.input.right) {
                bear.x += 3;
                bear.scaleX =  1;
            }

            //Frame settings
            if (!game.input.left && !game.input.right) {
                bear.frame = bear.anim[0];
            } else {
                bear.frame = bear.anim[bear.age %  bear.anim.length];
            }
        });
    };

    //Adds an apple
    game.addApple = function(x, speed) {
        //Create apple
        var apple = new Sprite(16, 16);
        apple.image = game.assets['http://enchantjs.com/assets/images/icon0.gif'];
        apple.x = x;
        apple.y = -16;
        apple.frame = 15;
        apple.speed = speed;
        game.rootScene.addChild(apple);

        //Periodic processing of the sprite
        apple.addEventListener(Event.ENTER_FRAME, function() {
            apple.y += apple.speed;
            //Collision with the bear

            //Collision with the ground
            else if (apple.y > 320 - 32) {
                game.rootScene.removeChild(apple);
            }
        });
    };
```

```
//Periodic processing of the scene
game.framesLeft = 10*game.fps; // 10 seconds
game.rootScene.addEventListener(Event.ENTER_FRAME, function() {
    game.framesLeft--;
    if (game.framesLeft > 0) {
        //Apple creation
        if ((game.frame % 10) === 0) {
            var x     = rand(300);
            var speed = 3 + rand(6);
            game.addApple(x,speed);
        }
        label.text = "Time left:" + Math.floor(game.framesLeft / game.fps)  +
            "<BR />Score:" + game.score;
    } else {
        //Display Game Over
        game.end(game.score, "Your score is " + game.score);
    }
});

//Start game
game.start();
};

//Generates a random number
function rand(num){
    return Math.floor(Math.random() * num);
}
```

If you run this code, you can move a bear around on the screen with a d-pad and see apples falling from the top of the screen. However, the start and game over screens don't appear yet. We show you how to add those screens in the following section.

Adding Required Plug-Ins

The start and game over screens appear automatically with the addition of the nineleap.enchant.js plug-in. Do the following to add it to the project:

1. Click on the drop-down menu at the top of the screen and choose index.html.

2. Type in the code in Listing 4-3 under <script src='/static/enchant.js-latest/ enchant.js'></script>.

   Listing 4-3. Adding the nineleap.enchant.js Plug-In

   ```
   <script src='/static/enchant.js-latest/plugins/nineleap.enchant.js'></script>
   ```

3. Click Run. The start and game over screens appear automatically due to the addition of the plug-in.

Creating Score-Sharing Screens

The score-sharing screen appears only if you upload your game to 9leap.net. This screen allows players to see their final scores and gives them the ability to share the score on Twitter via 9leap.net. To set up the game to use the score-sharing screen, do the following:

1. Near the end of the code, change game.end(); to what is shown in Listing 4-4.

   Listing 4-4. Using the Score-Sharing Screen

   ```
   game.end(game.score, "Your score is " + game.score);
   ```

Next, upload your game to 9leap.net. When you play your game, a screen should appear when the game is over that shows your score along with the message you specified (such as "Your score is...").

As you have seen, the start and game over screens are very easy to implement into your game, requiring just an additional plug-in. Adding this plug-in polishes your game and makes it easier for your players to understand the exact starting and ending points.

Using Collision Detection

As we have seen, our game involves having a bear character collect apples falling from the top of a screen. As far as the apples are concerned, we know how to create them, how to make them fall over time, and even how to make them disappear (removeChild()). However, we need some way to tell when our bear character comes in contact with an apple. To do this, we use specific methods, which are part of all entity objects.

Methods for Collision Detection

Table 4-2 shows the two methods used for collision detection. These methods are part of the Entity object, and as such can be called on practically anything within a scene.

Table 4-2. Collision Detection Methods

Method (Arguments)	Description
intersect(otherEntity)	Performs collision detection based on whether or not the bounding rectangles of the entities – the entity calling intersect() and the other entity - are intersecting. The other entity must have the properties x, y, width, and height.
within(otherEntity, distance)	Performs collision detection based on the distance between the central points of both entities.

Detecting Collisions with the within Method

The first collision detection method is `within()`. Do the following to implement it in the apple-catching game:

1. Beneath the line `//Collision with the bear`, type in the code in Listing 4-4.

    Listing 4-4. Using within()

    ```
    if (bear.within(apple, 16)) {
        game.score+=30;
        game.rootScene.removeChild(apple);
    }
    ```

This calculates the center point of the apple and the center point of the bear each frame, and then calculates the distance between the two. If the distance is 16 pixels or less, the game's score increases by 30 and the apple is removed from `rootScene`.

Detecting Collisions with the intersect Method

Another method exists for detecting collisions between objects. Do the following to see how to use the method:

1. Replace `bear.within(apple, 16)` in Listing 4-4 with `bear.intersect(apple)`.

This causes the program to look at the total area of both the bear and the apple. If those areas intersect at all, the score increases by 30 and the apple is removed from `rootScene`.

Collision detection is an important part of games. Catching an apple, shooting down a ship, or anything involving one sprite coming in contact with another require collision detection. If you run into any problems with the creation of the code in this section, you can find a fully working copy at `http://code.9leap.net/codes/show/27891`.

Creating an Interactive Map

We saw a rudimentary example of a map in Chapter 3, which copied a single tile across the screen, but further setup is required to create interactive maps in enchant.js. However, the principle is the same and still uses the `draw()` method to tile a given surface with map tiles.

In our sample code for this section, we create a simple maze program using a map. Our main character will be able to traverse only light-brown road tiles and will be unable to travel over the green grass tiles. The game ends once the main character reaches the treasure chest. Figures 4-4 and 4-5 illustrate this program.

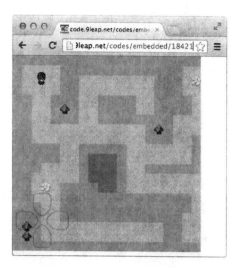

Figure 4-4. *Start screen of the Map Example project*

Figure 4-5. *End screen of the Map Example project*

Creating a Map Object

The first step to create a map is to create a Map object. Do the following to set up the game and create a Map object:

1. Fork the blank template from http://code.9leap.net/codes/show/27204 to have a project to enter your code into.

2. Type in the code in Listing 4-5 to set up the basics of the game.

Listing 4-5. Basics of the Sidescroller

```
var DIR_LEFT  = 0;
var DIR_RIGHT = 1;
var DIR_UP    = 2;
var DIR_DOWN  = 3;

enchant();
window.onload = function() {
    var game = new Core(320, 320);
    game.fps = 16;
    game.preload(
        'http://enchantjs.com/assets/images/map0.gif',
        'http://enchantjs.com/assets/images/chara0.gif');

    game.onload = function() {
        var player = new Sprite(32, 32);
        player.image = game.assets['http://enchantjs.com/assets/images/chara0.gif'];
        player.x = 2 * 16;
        player.y = 16;
        player.dir   = DIR_DOWN;
        player.anim  = [
             9, 10, 11, 10, //Left
            18, 19, 20, 19, //Right
            27, 28, 29, 28, //Up
             0,  1,  2,  1];//Down

            //Frame setting
            if (!game.input.up && !game.input.down &&
                !game.input.left && !game.input.right) player.age = 1;//Standing Still
            player.frame = player.anim[player.dir * 4 + (player.age % 4)];

        });

        var pad = new Pad();
        pad.y = 220;
        game.rootScene.addChild(pad);

    };
    game.start();
};
```

3. Under game.onload = function() {, type in the code in Listing 4-6 to create the Map
    object and assign the tile set image to it.

    Listing 4-6. Creating the Map Object

    ```
    var map = new Map(16, 16);
    map.image = game.assets['http://enchantjs.com/assets/images/map0.gif'];
    ```

Populating Tiles and Setting Collision

Now that you've created the map, you need to populate it with tiles. In an earlier example, we used a loop to populate all the tiles in a map with the same green grass tile. In this map, we use different tiles in a specific arrangement, so they must be manually entered. Do the following to copy and paste the tile data:

4. Copy the code from http://code.9leap.net/codes/show/27905 and insert it into the line after Listing 4-6. If you are not using 9leap, copy the code from Listing 4-7.

Listing 4-7. Loading in Tile Data

```
map.loadData([
[0,0,0,0,0,0,0,0,0,0,0,0,0,0,0,0,0,0,0,0,0,0,0,0],
[0,2,2,2,2,0,0,0,0,0,0,0,0,0,0,0,0,0,2,2,2,2,2,0],
[0,2,2,2,2,0,0,2,2,2,2,2,2,2,2,0,0,0,0,2,2,2,2,2,0],
[0,2,2,2,2,0,0,2,2,2,2,2,2,2,2,0,0,0,0,2,2,2,2,2,0],
[0,0,2,2,0,0,0,2,2,0,0,0,0,2,2,0,0,0,0,0,2,2,0,0,0],
[0,0,2,2,0,0,0,2,2,0,0,0,0,2,2,0,0,0,0,0,2,2,0,0,0],
[0,0,2,2,0,0,0,2,2,0,0,0,0,0,0,0,0,0,2,2,2,2,0,0,0],
[0,0,2,2,2,2,2,2,2,2,2,2,2,2,0,0,0,0,2,2,2,2,0,0,0],
[0,0,2,2,2,2,2,2,2,2,2,2,2,2,0,0,0,0,2,2,0,0,0,0,0],
[0,0,0,0,0,2,2,0,0,0,0,0,2,2,2,2,2,2,2,0,0,0,0,0],
[0,0,0,0,0,2,2,0,0,0,0,0,2,2,2,2,2,2,2,0,0,0,0,0],
[0,0,2,2,2,2,2,0,0,0,0,0,2,2,0,0,0,0,0,0,0,0,0,0],
[0,0,2,2,2,2,2,0,0,0,0,0,2,2,2,2,2,2,2,2,2,2,0,0],
[0,0,2,2,2,0,0,0,0,0,0,0,2,2,2,2,2,2,2,2,2,2,0,0],
[0,0,2,2,2,0,0,0,0,0,0,0,0,0,0,0,0,0,0,2,2,0,0,0],
[0,0,0,2,2,0,0,0,0,0,0,0,0,0,0,0,0,0,0,2,2,0,0,0],
[0,0,0,2,2,0,0,0,0,0,0,0,0,0,0,0,0,0,2,2,2,2,0,0],
[0,0,0,2,2,2,2,2,2,2,2,2,2,2,2,2,2,0,0,2,2,2,2,0],
[0,0,0,2,2,2,2,2,2,2,2,2,2,2,2,2,2,0,0,2,2,2,2,0],
[0,0,0,0,0,0,0,0,0,0,0,0,0,0,0,0,0,0,0,0,0,0,0,0]
],[
[-1,-1,-1,-1,-1,-1,-1,-1,-1,-1,-1,-1,-1,-1,-1,-1,-1,-1,-1,-1,-1,-1],
[-1,-1,-1,-1,-1,-1,-1,-1,-1,-1,-1,-1,-1,-1,-1,-1,-1,-1,-1,-1,-1,-1],
[-1,-1,-1,-1,-1,-1,-1,-1,-1,-1,-1,-1,-1,-1,-1,-1,-1,-1,18,-1,-1,-1],
[-1,-1,-1,-1,-1,-1,-1,-1,-1,-1,-1,-1,-1,-1,-1,-1,-1,-1,-1,-1,-1,-1],
[-1,-1,-1,-1,-1,-1,-1,-1,-1,-1,-1,-1,-1,-1,-1,-1,-1,-1,-1,-1,-1,-1],
[-1,-1,-1,-1,-1,23,-1,-1,-1,-1,-1,-1,-1,-1,-1,-1,-1,-1,-1,-1,-1,-1],
[-1,-1,-1,-1,-1,-1,-1,-1,-1,-1,-1,-1,-1,-1,-1,-1,-1,-1,-1,-1,-1,-1],
[-1,-1,-1,-1,-1,-1,-1,-1,-1,-1,-1,-1,-1,-1,-1,23,-1,-1,-1,-1,-1,23],
[-1,-1,-1,-1,-1,-1,-1,-1,-1,-1,-1,-1,-1,-1,-1,-1,-1,-1,-1,-1,-1,23],
[-1,-1,-1,-1,-1,-1,-1,-1,-1,-1,-1,-1,-1,-1,-1,-1,-1,-1,-1,-1,-1,-1],
[-1,-1,-1,-1,-1,-1,-1,-1, 1, 1, 1,-1,-1,-1,-1,-1,-1,-1,-1,-1,-1,-1],
[-1,-1,-1,-1,-1,-1,-1,-1, 1, 1, 1,-1,-1,-1,-1,-1,-1,-1,-1,-1,-1,-1],
[-1,-1,-1,-1,-1,-1,-1,-1, 1, 1, 1,-1,-1,-1,-1,-1,-1,-1,-1,-1,-1,-1],
[-1,-1,-1,18,-1,-1,-1,-1, 1, 1, 1,-1,-1,-1,-1,-1,-1,-1,-1,-1,-1,-1],
[-1,-1,-1,-1,-1,-1,-1,-1,-1,-1,-1,-1,-1,-1,-1,-1,-1,-1,-1,-1,-1,-1],
[-1,-1,-1,-1,-1,-1,-1,-1,-1,-1,-1,-1,-1,-1,-1,-1,-1,-1,-1,-1,-1,-1],
[-1,-1,-1,-1,-1,-1,-1,-1,-1,-1,-1,-1,-1,-1,-1,-1,-1,-1,-1,-1,-1,-1],
```

```
    [-1,23,-1,-1,-1,-1,-1,-1,-1,-1,-1,-1,-1,-1,-1,-1,-1,-1,-1,25,-1,-1],
    [-1,23,-1,-1,-1,-1,-1,-1,-1,-1,-1,-1,-1,-1,-1,-1,-1,-1,-1,-1,-1,-1],
    [-1,-1,-1,-1,-1,-1,-1,-1,-1,-1,-1,-1,-1,-1,-1,-1,-1,-1,-1,-1,-1,-1]
]);
```

This code shows how the loadData() function is used to populate a map. It is made up of two sections of arrays, separated by a closing bracket, a comma, and an opening bracket "],[". Because these are two separate groups, let's start by addressing the first of the two.

The first array group, which begins with [0,0,0,0...], specifies to start laying out the tile in the 1st position (the green grass tile) as the first row of the tiles map. These tiles come from the tile set image, which was assigned to map.image earlier. The tile size used (16x16) was designated when the map was first created with the Map object constructor (var map = new Map(16, 16);).

The closing bracket and comma after the first line of tile designations (...2,2,2,0),) specifies to begin a new row of tiles. This tiling process continues until we reach the "],[" about halfway through Listing 4-10.

We then begin the process again. This time, however, tiles specified will overlay whichever tile currently resides in the location specified to be tiled. A value of –1 means to not place any tile in the specified location. This layering technique allows objects such as flowers, trees, and the treasure chest to be placed on the map, over the green grass or tan road tiles.

■ **Note** It is quite labor intensive to manually input the 2-dimensional arrays defining the tile sequence for the map or the 2-dimensional array used for collision detection. To automatically create this data, enchant.js supports a map editor, and we recommend using that editor when you create a map for your games. You can find the map editor and instructions for using it at http://enchantjs.com/resource/the-map-editor/.

The next step is to specify collision on the map. On the map, there will be both green grass tiles and brown road tiles. The main character should be able to walk only on the brown road tiles, so we set collision to make this happen. This is set with another array, with 0 representing passable and 1 representing impassable, and specifies if the tile can be walked on by the character or not.

5. Create the collision data for the map by copying it from
    http://code.9leap.net/codes/show/27909 and pasting it beneath the loadData array
    you just entered. You can also copy it from Listing 4-8 if necessary.

Listing 4-8. Setting Collision Data

```
map.collisionData = [
    [1,1,1,1,1,1,1,1,1,1,1,1,1,1,1,1,1,1,1,1,1,1],
    [1,0,0,0,0,1,1,1,1,1,1,1,1,1,1,1,1,1,0,0,0,0,1],
    [1,0,0,0,0,1,1,0,0,0,0,0,0,0,0,1,1,1,0,0,0,0,1],
    [1,0,0,0,0,1,1,0,0,0,0,0,0,0,0,1,1,1,0,0,0,0,1],
    [1,1,0,0,1,1,1,0,0,1,1,1,1,0,0,1,1,1,1,0,0,1,1],
    [1,1,0,0,1,1,1,0,0,1,1,1,1,0,0,1,1,1,1,0,0,1,1],
    [1,1,0,0,1,1,1,0,0,1,1,1,1,1,1,1,1,1,0,0,0,0,1,1],
    [1,1,0,0,0,0,0,0,0,0,0,0,0,0,1,1,1,0,0,0,0,1,1],
    [1,1,0,0,0,0,0,0,0,0,0,0,0,0,1,1,1,0,0,1,1,1,1],
    [1,1,1,1,1,0,0,1,1,1,1,0,0,0,0,0,0,0,1,1,1,1],
    [1,1,1,1,1,0,0,1,1,1,1,0,0,0,0,0,0,0,1,1,1,1],
    [1,1,1,0,0,0,0,1,1,1,1,1,0,0,1,1,1,1,1,1,1,1,1],
    [1,1,0,0,0,0,0,1,1,1,1,1,0,0,0,0,0,0,0,0,0,1,1],
```

```
    [1,1,0,0,0,1,1,1,1,1,1,1,0,0,0,0,0,0,0,0,0,1,1],
    [1,1,0,0,0,1,1,1,1,1,1,1,1,1,1,1,1,1,1,1,0,0,1,1],
    [1,1,1,0,0,1,1,1,1,1,1,1,1,1,1,1,1,1,1,1,0,0,1,1],
    [1,1,1,0,0,1,1,1,1,1,1,1,1,1,1,1,1,1,1,0,0,0,0,1],
    [1,1,1,0,0,0,0,0,0,0,0,0,0,0,0,0,1,1,0,0,0,0,0,1],
    [1,1,1,0,0,0,0,0,0,0,0,0,0,0,0,0,1,1,0,0,0,0,0,1],
    [1,1,1,1,1,1,1,1,1,1,1,1,1,1,1,1,1,1,1,1,1,1,1,1]
];
```

Using Collision Detection for Movement

Now the map in our game exists, but we need a way to move our character around in accordance with the data. Maps in enchant.js support a method for finding out if a specific position on the map is able to be walked on or not. This is used to determine if the character can walk on the tile or not. Do the following to implement it:

1. Under the line player.anim = [...];//Down, type in the code in Listing 4-9.

Listing 4-9. Character Movement with Map Collision Detection

```
player.addEventListener(Event.ENTER_FRAME, function() {
    //Move up
    if (game.input.up) {
        player.dir = DIR_UP;
        player.y -= 4;
        if (map.hitTest(player.x + 16, player.y + 32)) player.y += 4;
    }
    //Move down
    else if (game.input.down) {
        player.dir = DIR_DOWN;
        player.y += 4;
        if (map.hitTest(player.x + 16, player.y + 32)) player.y -= 4;
    }
    //Move left
    else if (game.input.left) {
        player.dir = DIR_LEFT;
        player.x -= 4;
        if (map.hitTest(player.x + 16, player.y + 32)) player.x += 4;
    }
    //Move right
    else if (game.input.right) {
        player.dir = DIR_RIGHT;
        player.x += 4;
        if (map.hitTest(player.x + 16, player.y + 32)) player.x -= 4;
    }

    //Frame setting
    if (!game.input.up && !game.input.down &&
        !game.input.left && !game.input.right) player.age = 1;//Standing Still
    player.frame = player.anim[player.dir * 4 + (player.age % 4)];

});
```

The hitTest() method uses the data arrays we assigned to collisionData to find if an obstacle exists at a given XY coordinate on the map. Although this method will tell us if an obstacle exists at a given location on the map, we must manually specify what should be done if an obstacle does in fact exist.

This code is all inside a periodically processed event listener, so it executes with the occurrence of each new frame. The player character moves four pixels in the direction specified by the d-pad.

However, if the horizontal mid-point of the character borders a tile that contains an obstacle, the character cannot move any further in the direction of that obstacle. Did you notice how the nested if statements in Listing 4-12 increment the character's position in the opposite direction from whatever direction the movement is being handled for? By using the opposite calculation, the value of the character's position doesn't change, and the character remains stationary (if map.hitTest() returns true).

Scrolling the Map

The map we're using for our character is larger than the game screen, which means part of the map is obscured off the screen. When the character moves across the screen, the map should at some point scroll so the character can explore the entire map.

To make this happen, the first thing we need to do is combine the character and the map into a single unit, so both can be scrolled simultaneously. Do the following to make this happen:

1. Above var pad = new Pad();, combine the map and the player into a single Group by typing in the code in Listing 4-10.

    Listing 4-10. Combining the Map and Player into a Group

    ```
    var stage = new Group();
    stage.addChild(map);
    stage.addChild(player);
    game.rootScene.addChild(stage);
    ```

2. Set the map to scroll with the player by typing in the code in Listing 4-11 after game.rootScene.addChild(pad);.

    Listing 4-11. Scrolling the Map

    ```
    game.rootScene.addEventListener(Event.ENTER_FRAME, function(e) {
        //Set stage XY coordinates
        var x = Math.min((game.width  - 16) / 2 - player.x, 0);
        var y = Math.min((game.height - 16) / 2 - player.y, 0);
        x = Math.max(game.width,  x + map.width)  - map.width;
        y = Math.max(game.height, y + map.height) - map.height;
        stage.x = x;
        stage.y = y;
    });
    ```

This is probably easiest to understand if we look at how it is written in reverse.

First, we know that we are repositioning the stage group, which we created above, by assigning an x and y value to the stage's x and y positions. Keep in mind that stage contains both the map and the character and will move both of them simultaneously.

Next, we specify "subtract the width of the map from one of two values and assign it to x" (x = Math.max(game. width, x + map.width) - map.width;). The main concept to pay attention to here is that if the width of the game is greater than some other value (x + map.width), x will be assigned a value equal to the width of the game minus the width of the map. If the group is moved by this number (a negative number), the right edge of the map will line up with the right side of the game screen.

Finally, directly under the event listener declaration, we specify "either make the value of x zero, or a value equal to half of the game's width minus the current x position of the player (on the map)." If the character is on the map but has not moved to the right at least by an amount equal to half of the game screen, then zero gets assigned.

It's a bit complex, but the final result is that the map scrolls with the movement of the character in a way that always fills the game screen. You can see a simpler example of scrolling the background in the game "Heart_Runner" at http://9leap.net/games/3004, in which a player clicks the screen rapidly to make the character run through a forest that scrolls to the left behind the character.

Using Collision Detection for a Goal

At this point in the game the map and character should appear correctly. The character can be controlled with the d-pad and the map will scroll. However, if the character walks over the treasure chest, nothing happens. To have the game end, we must use collision detection in a different way.

We've seen how to perform collision detection between the two entities (intersect() or within()), and we've seen how to perform rudimentary collision detection to see if a character can move across a given tile. However, because the treasure chest, once tiled onto the map, doesn't have its own entity container, we can't use entity methods like intersect or within().

The treasure chest, for all intents and purposes, exists only as a set of coordinates on the map. To determine if the character is in contact with the treasure chest, we need to determine the distance between the location of the character and the location of the treasure chest on the map. Figure 4-6 shows this equation.

$$\text{Distance between 2 points} = \sqrt{(x_0 - x_1)^2 + (y_0 - y_1)^2}$$

Figure 4-6. *Distance formula*

Do the following to see how to create and use this formula:

1. Add the function to calculate the distance between two points on the map by typing in the code in Listing 4-12 at the very end of your existing code, outside the game.onload function.

   Listing 4-12. Creating a Function to Calculate Length

   ```
   function calcLen(x0, y0, x1, y1) {
       return Math.sqrt((x0 - x1) * (x0 - x1) + (y0 - y1) * (y0 - y1));
   }
   ```

The function Math.sqrt(), which calculates the square root of whatever value is passed as its argument, is a function of the Math object and can be called at any time in JavaScript.

2. Check if the character is touching the treasure chest panel by typing in the code in Listing 4-13 after `player.frame = player.anim[player.dir * 4 + (player.age % 4)];`.

Listing 4-13. Checking for Collision with the Treasure Chest

```
if (calcLen(player.x + 16, player.y + 16, 20 * 16 + 8, 17 * 16 + 8) <= 16) {
    game.end(0, "Goal");
}
```

Here, we are measuring the distance between the XY coordinates of the player sprite and the treasure chest. The "+16" and "+8" are there to have the program measure distance from the two objects based on the center of those objects instead of the top-left corner.

The multiplication used for the XY positions of the treasure chest (x1 & y1) uses the size of a single tile (16 pixels) times the number of tiles before the treasure chest tile to find the value of the x and y positions.

3. Click Run. The game ends when the character comes in contact with the treasure chest.

In this section, we created a game that enables a character to walk around on a map, but only on specific tiles. We also made the map scroll with the character's movement. Finally, we made the game end after the character reaches a treasure chest on the map. All these features and actions involved an interactive map. Interactive maps are great for two-dimensional games, especially two-dimensional role-playing games.

If you encounter any problems setting up the map in this section, you can find a complete and working code sample at `http://code.9leap.net/codes/show/23344`.

Implementing Sound

Our last advanced feature for this chapter is sound. Sound can be implemented in enchant.js for background music and events within the game, such as a ship shooting, a special ability being activated, and more to make your game immersive and interactive.

Our exercise for this section simply places several bananas on the screen, along with a single skull. If a player clicks a banana, the banana will disappear and a sound effect will play. If a player clicks the skull, the game will end. The goal of the game is to collect all the bananas. Figure 4-7 shows the starting state of this simple game. Figure 4-8 shows the game over screen.

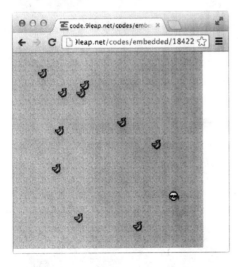

Figure 4-7. Banana game main screen

Figure 4-8. *Banana game end screen*

Downloading Sounds

Sounds, due to the nature of their large file size, are not included in the enchant.js package by default but can be downloaded from the same page. Do the following to download them:

1. Go to http://enchantjs.com and click Download. Download the zip file containing all sounds from the link at the very bottom of the page.

2. Play some of the sounds to see what is included in the file.

Setting Up the Game

For this example, we'll copy code for a complete game, and then implement sound into it. Do the following to set up the game:

1. Fork the code at http://code.9leap.net/codes/show/27917 for the complete game. If you are not using 9leap.net, copy and paste the code from Listing 4-14 into a blank enchant.js game.

Listing 4-14. Banana Game

```
enchant();
window.onload = function() {
    //Game object creation
    var game = new Core(320, 320);
    game.fps = 16;
    game.score = 0;
    game.bananaNum = 10;
    game.time = 0;
```

```
//Sound and image loading
game.preload(['se1.wav',
              'http://enchantjs.com/assets/images/icon0.gif',
              'http://enchantjs.com/assets/images/map0.gif']);

//Called when the loading is complete
game.onload = function() {

    //Background creation
    var bg = new Sprite(320, 320);
    var maptip = game.assets['http://enchantjs.com/assets/images/map0.gif'];
    var image = new Surface(320, 320);
    for (var j = 0; j < 320; j += 16) {
        for (var i = 0; i < 320; i += 16) {
            image.draw(maptip, 16 * 2, 0, 16, 16, i, j, 16, 16);
        }
    }
    bg.image = image;
    game.rootScene.addChild(bg);

    //Add bananas
    for (var k = 0; k < 10; k++) game.addBanana();

    //Add skull
    game.addDokuro();

    //Periodic scene processing
    game.rootScene.addEventListener(Event.ENTER_FRAME, function(){
        game.time ++;
    });
};

//Adds a skull
game.addDokuro = function(){
    var dokuro = new Sprite(16, 16);
    dokuro.x = rand(260) + 20;
    dokuro.y = rand(260) + 20;
    dokuro.image = game.assets['http://enchantjs.com/assets/images/icon0.gif'];
    dokuro.frame = 11;
    dokuro.addEventListener(Event.TOUCH_START, function(e) {
        game.end(0, "Game Over");
    });
    game.rootScene.addChild(dokuro);
};

//Adds a banana
game.addBanana = function(){
    var banana = new Sprite(16, 16);
    banana.x = rand(260) + 20;
    banana.y = rand(260) + 20;
    banana.image = game.assets['http://enchantjs.com/assets/images/icon0.gif'];
    banana.frame = 16;
```

```
                //Event handling when the banana is touched
                banana.addEventListener(Event.TOUCH_START, function(e) {
                    game.rootScene.removeChild(this);

                    game.bananaNum--;
                    if (game.bananaNum === 0){
                        game.end(1000000 - game.time,
                            (game.time / game.fps).toFixed(2) + " seconds to Clear!");
                    }
                });
                game.rootScene.addChild(banana);
            };

        //Start game
        game.start();
    };

    //Generates a random number
    function rand(num){
        return Math.floor(Math.random() * num);
    }
```

Loading Sounds

Just like when you are working with images, you can load sounds into memory by using the Core object's preload()
function. Although the Sound object supports loading directly with the load() method, we recommend loading your
sound elements with the preload() method, as it can prevent problems with players having to wait in-game for
elements to load if they are on a slow connection.

Once your elements are preloaded, they can be created as sound objects inside your game by using the Sound
object constructor. Do the following to see how:

1. After game.onLoad = function() {, type in the code in Listing 4-15.

   Listing 4-15. Creating a Sound Object

   ```
   game.se = game.assets['se1.wav'];
   ```

Playing Sounds

Once a sound object has been created, it can be played with a specific method:

1. After game.rootScene.removeChild(this);, type in the code in Listing 4-16.

   Listing 4-16. Playing a Sound

   ```
   game.se.play();
   ```

2. Click Run. When you click on a banana, a sound plays. Clicking the skull ends the game.

In this section, we created a game that plays a sound when a player clicks the bananas within the game. Sounds add an element of interactivity to your games, providing an additional element of sensory feedback for your players. It's easy to include sounds in your game by taking advantage of the free library of sounds available for download on the enchant.js home page.

Conclusion

Congratulations on making it through the advanced section! You should now understand the more advanced capabilities of enchant.js, including how scenes are organized and navigated in a game, how to create start and game over screens, how to implement maps and scroll them, and how to enable sound playback. These will allow you to add further levels of interactivity to your games, making them more engaging to your players.

In the next chapter, we step back from the specific functionality of enchant.js and take a look at game design. Making your own original games takes creativity, so we introduce you to a sample workflow you can use to create your own games, taking you through every step of the design process.

CHAPTER 5

Game Design

Up to this point, we've focused on the basics of JavaScript and enchant.js, including the specific format you must use to write your code to take advantage of the many features of enchant.js. These basics include sprites, labels, scenes, maps, how to upload and share your games on 9leap.net, and more. However, this alone does not a good game developer make!

If you dive right in and try to build your own game from scratch without any references, using only what we've previously covered in this book, you will encounter issues. Many issues. To make the entire process easier for you, we provide some background in this chapter about designing and developing games from scratch.

With great power (or features, rather) comes great responsibility, and as a game developer, you have a duty to your players. The enchant.js engine is a powerful tool for developing games. But what is its ultimate purpose? To bring happiness to the player, of course! Fun is the point of games. Your players are the ones who will be interacting with your game, and if they are not enjoying the experience, they won't be motivated to play the game you've invested time in to develop.

This chapter specifically covers the creative process of building an original game. It is full of hints about how to make this process simple. It also gives you tips about how to engineer your game to be appealing and entertaining to your players. We cover the development cycle a game should go through: from conception, to coding, and finally to improving the finished game.

Unbreakable Rules of Mini-Game Development

There are several "unbreakable" rules that you should follow when you make games with enchant.js. Most games developed with the library are mini-games. Mini-games are games on a small scale, defined by a short playing time and simple progression between levels.

Usually, they require only one to three people for development and sometimes can be created in less than an hour. Although some are developed over a few days, you should not spend much more than this on a single game. Keep trying and don't worry about failure. The more you make mistakes and learn from them, the more your skills will increase.

Don't Try to Make an Epic Game

You're looking at guaranteed failure if you try to make an epic game right from the start. Begin by making a small, simple game that fits your skills and then gradually expand its features. In fact, most of the previous financially successful games did not begin with the goal of creating an epic game. If you take a closer look at those games, you will find that they are composed of extremely simple components, albeit many of them.

Within a completed simple game, many stages exist, and every stage is connected to another by a single story. Games in which the rules are complicated from the outset are rare.

Don't Try to Make a Completely Original Game

It's important that you don't try to achieve 100% originality when you make the rules of your game. Games have been developed, in one form or another, for a very long time. Many beginners set out eager to make something no one has seen before, but they run the risk of creating something that, in fact, no one enjoys. Try imagining a food that no one has tasted or heard of before. Now imagine eating such a food, prepared by someone who has never cooked before. A frightening thought, isn't it?

It might turn out to be a delicacy by sheer luck, but good food doesn't usually deviate much from the adjectives we're used to hearing to describe them: sweet, spicy, juicy, hearty, and so on. Sure, a master chef works with these flavors and integrates them in new and innovative ways, but you don't see those who are just starting to study the art of cooking going head first into a culinary science experiment.

Innovation is important, but it's not worth it if the flavor ends up terrible. Consider peanut butter and jelly. It's better to combine two familiar flavors into something new than trying to cook something entirely unheard of. Games are the same. Don't aim for originality right from the start. Combine familiar themes and rules, and then gradually start creating your own unique twist from there.

Players Should Grasp the Game in Ten Seconds

People get easily discouraged by complex games with many rules. In a perfect game, players instinctually grasp how the game works and get hooked the instant they start playing. You have to make the players think "This is fun!" in ten seconds or less. Don't expect your players to be patient. They should see as much of the game and its appeal as possible from the moment they start playing.

If your game has multiple levels or is more complex than a standard mini-game, consider adding an optional tutorial level to the beginning of your game. Tutorial levels are great ways to teach your players how to play while retaining a hands-on feel.

Don't Get Too Absorbed in Programming

Programming is fun in and of itself, and some games possess a fascinating structure. That being said, it's easy to overly focus on the programming and lose sight of the essence of the game. Remember that your final goal is to create something that many people will play. Keep your focus on making the game fun, not on the complexities of its programming.

When in Trouble, Go "Time Attack"

In most games, you can up the ante and the fun simply by adding a time limit (time attack). For instance, in "High Speed Reversi," posted to 9leap (http://9leap.net/games/4), a simple Reversi (Othello) game takes on new life simply by gaining a time limit. It takes a slow-paced game of strategy and raises the stakes and difficulty considerably.

Don't Get Caught Up in What's Missing

It's typical for game developers to be short on time and resources, even when a large-scale game is being developed by a massive company. Unlimited development time and resources is a virtually impossible concept. The moment you start fretting about a lack of time or resources is the moment your game's progress grinds to a halt. Instead, focus on making the best game possible with the time and resources available.

Make it Fun for Others

The entire point of creating a game is to create something fun for others. If you've gone to all the trouble of making a game, don't get hung up on how many people download it or how elite it is. Start by trying to bring a smile to your friends and family with your game.

Game Development Process

Games undoubtedly come in many forms, and it is always a good idea to investigate some of the different kinds of games, such as Fruits Panic (an action puzzle game at 9leap.net/games/90) or Golf Solitaire (a card game at 9leap.net/games/2994) for inspiration when you're planning to make your own games in enchant.js.

However, once you've settled on the general type of game you are interested in making, how you go about actually creating it can be a chaotic process if you don't have a roadmap to point you in the right direction. The following list shows six steps for developing your own game. Please note that game design is a very large topic with many differing opinions. Because most of the games created with enchant.js are simple, the development process listed here might differ from more complex methodologies.

1. Design the game's rules.

    a. When you're just starting with your first game, it can be a bit confusing to create all the rules from scratch by yourself. For example, if you are designing a game like "Block Breaker," you need to decide how the ball will change direction when hitting a block versus hitting a paddle, decide on all the power-ups, the speed of the ball, the rate at which the ball speeds up, and more. In this case, it is a very good idea to see how others have implemented rules for their own games and imitate their techniques. The games you should use as models during this process are ones you feel able to make yourself. Sketch your ideas on paper and even simulate a few actions if you can. Don't worry if you don't have all the details yet. Don't overdo it.

2. Pick a theme and prepare sprites.

    a. Choose a general idea of the kind of game you'd like to make. Take a minute to visualize your game. Will it be racing cars? Spaceships battling aliens? What will stick with the players afterwards? You've already decided the rules of your game, so perhaps it's good to think of a theme that will maximize the players' potential. You should also assess your art, sound, and story assets that go with the theme. How will you create or acquire them?

3. Program the game.

    a. You've already picked out your theme and rules, so now it's time to code the game based on them. Depending on your theme, you may have to prepare basic graphics, sounds, or story before doing this.

4. Play it yourself.

    a. Once a version of your game has been programmed, it's essential to try it out yourself. No matter how carefully you lay out your game rules, if you don't really test the game you will miss problems in your rules. You're not just testing to see whether or not your game follows the rules you've established. You're also repeatedly testing for balance, to see if the game is too hard, too easy, or too difficult to control. Get help from others if you can. The more people play it and give you feedback, the more you can learn how to make it more fun.

5. Refine your rules and return to Step 3.

    a. After testing your game a bit, reexamine your rules, see how they can be improved, change your code to implement the improvements, and then play your game again. Repeat this formula as often as necessary. The game's final level of interest will vary greatly depending on how carefully you do this. If you're pleased with what you've come up with, it might be a good idea to add more levels.

6. Finish the game.

    a. Here's where you add the finishing touches. For example, make a title screen, add a high-score ranking table, and refine the appearance of the game.

If you already have an idea for the kind of game you want to make, feel free to exchange Step 1 and Step 2. It can be fun to pick a theme first and then cook up rules to go with it.

In actual game development, this procedure is much more complicated and varies depending on the production process. However, due to the features provided by enchant.js, the development cycle is reduced to a point where you can repeat this cycle of game development much more quickly than without the use of the library.

Try coming up with a game you'd like to develop. In the following sections, we go through the development process step-by-step, making a full sample game from start to finish. As we go through the process, try to find ways of utilizing the process for your own game's development.

Design the Rules of the Game

In reality, you can begin to design your game either by deciding the rules of the game or by deciding on a theme for your game. However, if you are a beginner to game development we recommend you plan the rules first because implementing the rules that govern a game is the biggest obstacle for beginning game programmers.

You might wonder, "How do you come up with the rules of a game?" Well, putting it bluntly, you look at what's already out there first. Pick out something similar to your concept that matches your skill level. In the short but prolific history of computer games, you'll find that practically every rule in gaming has been repeatedly experimented on, polished, and transformed into an existing game. Just as in martial arts, games have certain predefined styles and techniques. Don't worry about innovating at this point.

Consider downloading an open source game from 9leap.net and then restructuring the source code, or examine the source code and use it as inspiration for implementing similar rules in your own game. Do not feel bad about borrowing the core rules of your game from an existing game. Even if you do this in the beginning, by adding new elements to the game bit by bit, your personality and individuality as a game designer will start to come through.

Whack-A-Mole, shooting games, dialogue-based role-playing games (RPGs), and puzzle games are some popular genres for beginners to imitate. If you're planning on making a game specifically for smartphones, we suggest starting with a puzzle or Whack-A-Mole game.

In the following sections, we use Whack-A-Mole as the basis for creating a new game. If by chance you're not familiar with it, Whack-A-Mole is a game where the goal is to hit moles as they appear out of their holes. It's a simple game and is good for beginners.

To begin, visit http://code.9leap.net/codes/show/23694 and play the game. Briefly look at the code as well to familiarize yourself with it, but you do not need to copy anything just yet.

Pick a Theme

An authentic Whack-A-Mole game uses an image of a mole. However, instead of a mole let's use an image of a Droid (Android) character. The Droid image is licensed under the Creative Commons license, so we're free to use it how we wish.

So for this game we'll make a Whack-A-Droid game instead of a Whack-A-Mole game. As you can see, there's absolutely nothing wrong with picking a theme after picking your rules. The important thing is to start out with something easy.

Of course, if you like drawing, you're welcome to draw a mole or something (or even someone) to get whacked. Simply by changing your theme, the essence of the game itself can change dramatically. Even if the logic of the game remains the same, by changing one little visual aspect, the entire game experience can change dramatically.

After you pick your theme, sketch on paper what your game will look like. It doesn't have to be a good sketch. When you lay out the elements of the game on paper it can help you understand the steps you need to take to create it. Figure 5-1 shows a sketch for our Whack-A-Droid game.

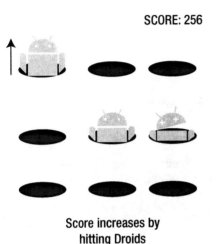

Figure 5-1. *Sketching your game*

The sketch shows a 3x3 grid of holes from which Droids will appear. Multiple Droids will appear out of the holes over time, and when a player clicks on them, they will grimace and then drop back down into the hole. On each successful hit, the player's score will increase. After a specified amount of time or specified number of Droids has appeared, the game will end.

It's perfectly fine to deviate from this sketch and provide an explanation when you get to the coding stage, but having something down on paper gives you a starting point to work from. After this, you can move on to creating your images if necessary.

To make the image file for the Droid (Figure 5-2), we used the free, open-source image editing program GIMP for Mac, which can be downloaded from www.gimp.org. However, you can use any image editing program to create sprite sheets.

Figure 5-2. *Droid character sprite sheet (mogura.png)*

In this sprite sheet, six frames of 48x48 pixels each are lined up from left to right (each image of a hole makes up a frame here), and then used when we create our sprite with Sprite(48,48). This coordinates with the size of one frame in this image, 48x48 pixels. In the first frame the Droid's face hasn't appeared yet, which he slowly does in the animation over the next four frames, leading up to the last frame that is shown when he gets whacked.

If you are using GIMP, you can do the following to create a very simple sprite sheet, such as the one shown in Figure 5-2:

1. Download or draw the components of your sprite sheet separately.

2. Create a new image the size of one frame.

3. Paste the components of your sprite sheet into the image.

4. Save the image as a separate file in PNG format to preserve transparency.

5. Edit the image to create the next frame and save it as a new image.

6. Repeat this process until you have created all desired frames.

7. Combine all of the images using the fuse layers script, included with GIMP. You can find instructions for using the fuse layers script at http://imagine.kicbak.com/blog/?p=114.

8. Save your image as a new PNG file.

The difference between each frame is important. If your frames are drastically different, then the animation would look robotic or nonexistent. In our Droid game, if one frame has an empty hole and the next frame has the Droid fully out of the hole, there would be no animation when the game runs and rapidly switches between the two frames. The Droid would suddenly appear. However, if there were 30 frames with the Droid moving up by a miniscule amount each time, this would not be an effective use of your file and would take more work to program. There is no specific number of frames you should make here. It is best to work with it to find out what looks best while not using too many frames for the job.

Program the Game

Once you've decided on the rules and theme of your game, it's time to move on to the programming stage. When you get to this step, the easiest way to start programming is by creating the simplest version of your game possible. This version does not need to be a working version necessarily, and definitely does not need to have all the features of the prospective game.

Creating the Simplest Version

The simplest version of a Whack-A-Mole game is a program that displays a single hole. Because eventually there will be more than one hole, we should first make a class for holes. Do the following to create this class:

1. Fork the blank project template at http://code.9leap.net/codes/show/28286. This template contains no game code but does contain the sprite sheet image you will need.

2. Initialize the enchant library and define a class for holes by typing in the code in Listing 5-1 into your project. This will run all the code inside it whenever a Pit object (hole) is created.

Listing 5-1. Defining the Pit Class

```
enchant();

Pit = Class.create(Sprite,{
    initialize:function(x,y){
        //Call the Sprite class (super class) constructor
        enchant.Sprite.call(this,48,48);
        this.image = game.assets['mogura.png'];
        this.x = x;
        this.y = y;
    }
});
```

3. Create a single hole on the screen by adding the code in Listing 5-2 under the code you just entered.

Listing 5-2. Creating a Hole on the Screen

```
window.onload = function(){
    game = new Game(320, 320);
    //Load Droid image
    game.preload('mogura.png');
    game.onload = function(){
        var pit = new Pit(100,100);
        game.rootScene.addChild(pit);
    }
    game.start();
}
```

4. Click Run. A hole is displayed, as shown in Figure 5-3. The Pit class we created extends the enchant.js Sprite class, and therefore can be used in the same way as Sprite. If you encounter problems, you can see the result of this step on code.9leap.net (http://code.9leap.net/codes/show/23728).

Figure 5-3. *Result of the simple Whack-A-Mole program*

Making the Droid Appear

The next step is to modify our `Pit` class to cause the Droid to appear. The only part of the code that changes is the `Pit` class, so we'll show only that section. Do the following to change the class:

1. Modify the `Pit` class to change to the next frame of the Droid if the current frame is one of the first four by modifying the `Pit` class to match Listing 5-3. This loops the animation of the Droid appearing over and over again, but it is the groundwork for the next few steps. In this and all future code listings in the chapter, changes from the previous code are in boldface.

Listing 5-3. Updated Pit Class

```
Pit = Class.create(Sprite,{
    initialize:function(x,y){
        //Call the Sprite class (super class) constructor
        enchant.Sprite.call(this,48,48);
        this.image = game.assets['mogura.png'];
        this.x = x;
        this.y = y;
```

```
        //Defines an event listener to run every frame
        this.addEventListener('enterframe',this.tick);
    },
    tick:function(){
        this.frame++;
        //Loop the animation once complete
        if(this.frame>=4)this.frame=0;
    }
});
```

2. Click Run. The Droid repeatedly appears out of the hole, as shown in Figure 5-4. If you encounter problems, you can check the result of this step on code.9leap.net (http://code.9leap.net/codes/edit/23729).

Figure 5-4. *Whack-A-Mole updated with animation*

Adjusting the Animation Speed

We've created an animation of our little Droid quickly appearing from his hole. However, he moves too fast to be able to hit him, so we need to slow him down a bit. Currently, after the fourth frame of the Droid sprite we return immediately to frame 0. This sudden return to his hole feels unnatural. Let's rewrite it so that once we progress to the fourth frame, we go backwards back down to 0. Do the following to make these changes:

1. Add a variable mode to the Pit class. Use it to define how the Droid should behave with respect to animation by modifying the Pit class to match Listing 5-4.

   Listing 5-4. Animating the Pit Class

```
Pit = Class.create(Sprite,{
    initialize:function(x,y){
        //Call the Sprite class (super class) constructor
        enchant.Sprite.call(this,48,48);
        this.image = game.assets['mogura.png'];
        this.x = x;
        this.y = y;
        //Defines an event listener to run every frame
        this.addEventListener('enterframe',this.tick);
        //Keeps track of the state of the Droid
        this.mode = 0;
    },
    tick:function(){
        //only change the frame every other frame
        //the return call ends the function
        if(game.frame%2!=0)return;
        switch(this.mode){
            //Droid is appearing from the hole
            case 0:
                this.frame++;
                //change mode after completely appearing
                if(this.frame>=4) this.mode=1;
                break;
            //Droid is hiding in the hole
            case 1:
                this.frame--;
                //change mode after completely hiding
                if(this.frame<=0) this.mode=0;
                break;
        }
    }
});
```

If the mode is set to 0, which will represent the Droid in the process of appearing, but not fully having appeared, then the Droid will progress through the first four frames and then change its mode to 1. Mode 1 represents the Droid hiding in the hole and causes the Droid to reverse the order of frames it used while appearing. The end result is that the Droid will appear and then disappear repeatedly.

Our animation also has become a little cleaner. We've changed the code so frame processing happens every two frames, instead of every frame, based on an if statement, which makes it nice and smooth. Furthermore, we've added a new property called mode, with mode 0 (appearing) and mode 1 (in the process of hiding), and we've performed a switch based on that property to execute the corresponding handling. If you encounter problems, you can check the result of this step on code.9leap.net (http://code.9leap.net/codes/show/23730).

Making a Droid Appear Randomly

With our current code, if we make copies of the hole, all Droids would appear at the exact same time. We need to make the timing of the Droids' appearances random. Currently we have only mode 0 (appearing) and mode 1 (hiding), so we need to add a mode for waiting for a random amount of time between the two by doing the following:

1. Upgrade the Pit class to cause random time to elapse between appearing and disappearing by replaying the Pit class with the code shown in Listing 5-5.

Listing 5-5. Upgrading the Pit Class

```
//function to generate random numbers
rand = function(n){
    return Math.floor(Math.random()*n);
}

//Define a class for holes
Pit = Class.create(Sprite,{
    initialize:function(x,y){
        //Call the Sprite class (super class) constructor
        enchant.Sprite.call(this,48,48);
        this.image = game.assets['mogura.png'];
        this.x = x;
        this.y = y;
        //Defines an event listener to run every frame
        this.addEventListener('enterframe',this.tick);
        //Set the Droid mode to 2 (waiting) in the beginning.
        this.mode = 2;
        //Set the next mode as 0 (appearing)
        this.nextMode = 0;
        //wait for a random number (0-99) of frames
        this.waitFor =  game.frame+rand(100);
    },
    tick:function(){
        //only change the frame every other frame
        //the return call ends the function
        if(game.frame%2!=0)return;
        switch(this.mode){
            //Droid is appearing from the hole
            case 0:
                this.frame++;
                if(this.frame>=4) {
                //switch to Mode 2 (waiting) after appearing
                    this.mode=2;
                //the mode to go to after Mode 2 is Mode 1 (hide)
                this.nextMode=1;
                //Set a random waiting time for 0 ~ 99 frames
                this.waitFor = game.frame+rand(100);
                                }
```

```
                    break;
            //Droid is going to hide in the hole
            case 1:
                  this.frame--;
                  //if Droid is hidden...
                  if(this.frame<=0){
                        //Switch to Mode 2 (waiting)
                        this.mode=2;
                        //The next mode should be Mode 0 (appear)
                        this.nextMode=0;
                        //Set a random waiting time for 0 ~ 99 frames
                        this.waitFor = game.frame+rand(100);
                  }
                  break;
            //Droid is waiting
            case 2:
                  //if the game's current frame is greater than
                  //the set frame to wait for...
                  if(game.frame>this.waitFor){
                        //Make a transition to the next mode
                        this.mode = this.nextMode;
                  }
                  break;
        }
      }
});
```

We've added a function called rand() for generating random numbers and have also created a new mode, Mode 2 (waiting).

The number of frames that have elapsed since the start of the game is stored in game.frame. When the frame number set in waitFor has passed, we make a transition to the next mode. By inserting this between mode 0 (appearing) and mode 1 (hiding), the amount of time between the Droid's appearance and disappearance can be randomized.

If you have any problems, check the code at http://code.9leap.net/codes/show/23731.

Implementing Droid Whacking

So far we've set our Droid friend to randomly appear and disappear. Now let's create the handling for when he is clicked by the player. For the so-called "whacked" event, we use a touchstart event listener (event listeners are covered in Chapter 2). Do the following to implement it:

1. Modify the Pit class by adding the bold sections of code shown in Listing 5-6.

   Listing 5-6. Implementing the "Whacked" State

```
//Define a class for holes
Pit = Class.create(Sprite,{
      initialize:function(x,y){
            //Call the Sprite class (super class) constructor
            enchant.Sprite.call(this,48,48);
            this.image = game.assets['mogura.png'];
            this.x = x;
```

```
        this.y = y;
        //Defines an event listener to run every frame
        this.addEventListener('enterframe',this.tick);
        //Defines an event listener for when the Droid gets whacked
        this.addEventListener('touchstart',this.hit);
        //Set the Droid mode to 2 (waiting) in the beginning.
        this.mode = 2;
        //Set the next mode as 0 (appearing)
        this.nextMode = 0;
        //wait for a random number (0-99) of frames
        this.waitFor =  game.frame+rand(100);
    },
    tick:function(){
        //only change the frame every other frame
        //the return call ends the function
        if(game.frame%2!=0)return;
        switch(this.mode){
            //Droid is appearing from the hole
            case 0:
                this.frame++;
                if(this.frame>=4) {
                //switch to Mode 2 (waiting) after appearing
                    this.mode=2;
                //the mode to go to after Mode 2 is Mode 1 (hide)
                this.nextMode=1;
                //Set a random waiting time for 0 ~ 99 frames
                this.waitFor = game.frame+rand(100);
                        }
                break;
            //Droid is going to hide in the hole
            case 1:
                this.frame--;
                //if Droid is hidden...
                if(this.frame<=0){
                    //Switch to Mode 2 (waiting)
                    this.mode=2;
                    //The next mode should be Mode 0 (appear)
                    this.nextMode=0;
                    //Set a random waiting time for 0 ~ 99 frames
                    this.waitFor = game.frame+rand(100);
                }
                break;
            //Droid is waiting
            case 2:
                //if the game's current frame is greater than
                //the set frame to wait for...
                if(game.frame>this.waitFor){
                    //Make a transition to the next mode
                    this.mode = this.nextMode;
                }
                break;
```

```
                }
        },
        //Whack Droid
        hit:function(){
                //only when Droid has appeared at least half-way
                if(this.frame>=2){
                        //Droid after being whacked
                        this.frame=5;
                        //Switch to waiting mode
                        this.mode=2;
                        this.nextMode=1;
                        //Number of frames to wait is fixed at 10
                        this.waitFor = game.frame+10;
                }
        }
});
```

Take note of the new function hit we've just added. If you tap the Droid when at least half of his face has appeared, the whack animation will play.

After the whacked Droid frame has been displayed for ten frames, the Droid once again makes a transition to mode 1 (hiding). A program that switches states while implementing other functions in this way is called a *state machine*.

If you experience an unexpected behavior with your own code you can check the result of this step at http://code.9leap.net/codes/show/23739.

We've now created the essentials of a Whack-A-Mole game in which you antagonize our Droid friend. However, we still have a problem. If you continuously keep hitting the Droid, his face will get stuck in the whacked state.

Preventing Continuous Droid Whacking

We need to ensure that once the Droid has been whacked, we can't hit him again and keep him in the whacked state. For this purpose, let's add a new property to our Pit class to achieve this by doing the following:

1. Update the Pit class by adding the bold sections from Listing 5-7.

Listing 5-7. Preventing Looped Hit Animation

```
//Define a class for holes
Pit = Class.create(Sprite,{
    initialize:function(x,y){
        //Call the Sprite class (super class) constructor
        enchant.Sprite.call(this,48,48);
        this.image = game.assets['mogura.png'];
        this.x = x;
        this.y = y;
        //Defines an event listener to run every frame
        this.addEventListener('enterframe',this.tick);
        //Defines an event listener for when the Droid gets whacked
        this.addEventListener('touchstart',this.hit);
        //Set the Droid mode to 2 (waiting) in the beginning.
        this.mode = 2;
        //Set the next mode as 0 (appearing)
        this.nextMode = 0;
```

```
        //wait for a random number (0-99) of frames
        this.waitFor = game.frame+rand(100);
        //stores info on whether or not the Droid
        //has already been whacked
        this.currentlyWhacked = false;
    },
    tick:function(){
        //only change the frame every other frame
        //the return call ends the function
        if(game.frame%2!=0)return;
        switch(this.mode){
            //Droid is appearing from the hole
            case 0:
                this.frame++;
                if(this.frame>=4) {
                //switch to Mode 2 (waiting) after appearing
                this.mode=2;
                //the mode to go to after Mode 2 is Mode 1 (hide)
                this.nextMode=1;
                //Set a random waiting time for 0 ~ 99 frames
                this.waitFor = game.frame+rand(100);
                    }
                break;
            //Droid is going to hide in the hole
            case 1:
                this.frame--;
                //if Droid is hidden...
                if(this.frame<=0){
                    //Switch to Mode 2 (waiting)
                    this.mode=2;
                    //The next mode should be Mode 0 (appear)
                    this.nextMode=0;
                    //Set a random waiting time for 0 ~ 99 frames
                    this.waitFor = game.frame+rand(100);
                    //reset flag as the whacked Droid disappears
                    this.currentlyWhacked = false;
                }
                break;
            //Droid is waiting
            case 2:
                //if the game's current frame is greater than
                //the set frame to wait for...
                if(game.frame>this.waitFor){
                    //Make a transition to the next mode
                    this.mode = this.nextMode;
                }
                break;
        }
    },
    //Whack Droid
    hit:function(){
```

```
//Do nothing if the Droid has already been whacked
if(this.currentlyWhacked)return;
//only when Droid has appeared at least half-way
if(this.frame>=2){
        //Set the flag so we know he's been whacked
        this.currentlyWhacked = true;
        //Droid after being whacked
        this.frame=5;
        //Switch to waiting mode
        this.mode=2;
        this.nextMode=1;
        //Number of frames to wait is fixed at 10
        this.waitFor = game.frame+10;
    }
  }
});
```

Here, we added the `currentlyWhacked` property, a flag that indicates if the Droid has been whacked. When the Droid is created, this property is set to `false`. Whenever a Droid is whacked, this property gets set to `true` and begins the hiding animation sequence. After the Droid disappears, this flag gets set to `false` because a new Droid will come out of the hole. With this, we avoid a situation where the Droid can be continuously whacked.

If you are having problems writing your code to match this example, you can check the code at `http://code.9leap.net/codes/show/23740`.

Duplicating the Hole

We have almost completed the foundation of a working Whack-a-Droid game with just one hole. You may think, "Why did we go to all that trouble to create just one hole?" By creating a class as we did, we can complete our game in the blink of an eye. Do the following to replicate the hole:

1. Modify the `game.onload` function by editing it to match Listing 5-8.

   Listing 5-8. Replicating the Droid Hole

```
game.onload = function(){
        //Line up holes in a 4x4 matrix
        for(var y=0;y<4;y++){
            for(var x=0;x<4;x++){
                var pit = new Pit(x*48+20,y*48+20);
                game.rootScene.addChild(pit);
            }
        }
    }
```

2. Click Run. A line of Droids appears, as shown in Figure 5-5.

Figure 5-5. *Creating multiple instances of the* Pit *class*

And just like that, we have a Whack-A-Mole game! As you can see, using classes can be a massive timesaver.

Because we'll be refining our game further in the next steps, make sure everything you've done up to this point has gone successfully. The code up to this point can be examined, and forked, from http://code.9leap.net/codes/show/23741.

Randomly Lining Up Holes

When developing your game, it can be helpful to try out different approaches. For instance, to examine how it would affect the game, you might want to try making the holes in our Whack-A-Droid game appear randomly on the screen instead of lining up in a 4x4 grid. You can see the changes to make this happen in Listing 5-9 and Figure 5-6.

Listing 5-9. Placing Holes Randomly

```
game.onload = function(){
    for(var i=0;i<7;i++){
        //Place pits randomly
        var pit = new Pit(rand(300),rand(300));
        game.rootScene.addChild(pit);
    }
}
```

Figure 5-6. *Placing holes randomly*

Because the positions of the holes are random, they change each time you reload the game. Regardless of where the holes end up, they work the exact same way because they are defined by the Pit class.

Now it's time for the fun part. Depending on where the holes end up, the essence of the game will change. Put your creativity to work and try to create your own original hole arrangement. You've now completed your first game prototype!

Playing, Repeating, Completing

Once you have a working prototype, the next step is to play the prototype and note any parts of the game that need to be improved or added.

If you play our completed Whack-A-Droid game a few times, you'll notice two important things are missing: a score and a limit to the number of times the Droid appears.

If you tried making the holes for the game random, for the following examples reset your game.onload function back to what is displayed in Listing 5-8.

Displaying a Score

Let's start by displaying a score:

1. Create the ScoreLabel class by adding the code shown in Listing 5-10 above the line of code starting with window.onload.

Listing 5-10. ScoreLabel Class

```
//ScoreLabel class definition, extending Label class
ScoreLabel = Class.create(Label,{
    initialize:function(x,y){
        //Call the Label class constructor
        enchant.Label.call(this,"SCORE:0");
        this.x=x;
        this.y=y;
        this.score = 0;
    },
    //Adds points to the score
    add:function(pts){
        this.score+=pts;
        //Change the displayed score
        this.text="SCORE:"+this.score;
    }
});
```

2. Create a new instance of the ScoreLabel class by adding a new instance of the ScoreLabel class, as shown in Listing 5-11.

Listing 5-11. Creating a ScoreLabel

```
game.onload = function(){

    //Display ScoreLabel
    scoreLabel=new ScoreLabel(5,5);
    game.rootScene.addChild(scoreLabel);

    //Line up holes in a 4x4 matrix
    for(var y=0;y<4;y++){
        for(var x=0;x<4;x++){
            var pit = new Pit(x*48+20,y*48+20);
            game.rootScene.addChild(pit);
        }
    }
}
```

3. Add code to increase the score whenever a Droid gets hit by adding the bold sections from Listing 5-12 to the hit function.

Listing 5-12. Increasing the Score on a Hit

```
//Whack Droid
hit:function(){
        //Do nothing if the Droid has already been whacked
        if(this.currentlyWhacked)return;
        //only when Droid has appeared at least half-way
        if(this.frame>=2){
                //Set the flag so we know he's been whacked
                this.currentlyWhacked = true;
                //Droid after being whacked
                this.frame=5;
                //Switch to waiting mode
                this.mode=2;
                this.nextMode=1;
                //Number of frames to wait is fixed at 10
                this.waitFor = game.frame+10;
                //Add score
                scoreLabel.add(1);
        }
}
```

4. Click Run. A score appears in the upper-left side of the screen and increases by one whenever a player whacks a Droid.

If you encounter problems while adding this code, check the example code at http://code.9leap.net/codes/show/23777.

Limiting Droid Appearances

Things are looking close to being finished now that we've added a score. However, our Droid appears a bit too frequently, to the point where a good score can be achieved just by hitting the same spot rapidly. There's an inexhaustible supply of Droids, robbing the player of a challenging game experience.

Let's alter our game so our Droid appears only 30 times. Changing it this way forces players to get as many hits as they can during the 30 appearances of the Droid. Do the following to achieve this:

1. Create a variable for the total number of Droids and the maximum number of appearances for a Droid, and then implement them by copying in the bold sections from Listing 5-13.

Listing 5-13. Limiting Droid Appearances

```
enchant();
//function to generate random numbers
rand = function(n){
        return Math.floor(Math.random()*n);
}

//Number of appearances of the Droid
maxDroid = 30;
```

```
//Total number of Droids
totalDroid = 16;

//Define a class for holes
Pit = Class.create(Sprite,{
    initialize:function(x,y){
        //Call the Sprite class (super class) constructor
        enchant.Sprite.call(this,48,48);
        this.image = game.assets['mogura.png'];
        this.x = x;
        this.y = y;
        //Defines an event listener to run every frame
        this.addEventListener('enterframe',this.tick);
        //Defines an event listener for when the Droid gets whacked
        this.addEventListener('touchstart',this.hit);
        //Set the Droid mode to 2 (waiting) in the beginning.
        this.mode = 2;
        //Set the next mode as 0 (appearing)
        this.nextMode = 0;
        //wait for a random number (0-99) of frames
        this.waitFor =  game.frame+rand(100);
        //stores info on whether or not the Droid
        //has already been whacked
        this.currentlyWhacked = false;
    },
    tick:function(){
        //only change the frame every other frame
        //the return call ends the function
        if(game.frame%2!=0)return;
        switch(this.mode){
            //Droid is appearing from the hole
            case 0:
                this.frame++;
                if(this.frame>=4) {
                //switch to Mode 2 (waiting) after appearing
                this.mode=2;
                //the mode to go to after Mode 2 is Mode 1 (hide)
                this.nextMode=1;
                //Set a random waiting time for 0 ~ 99 frames
                this.waitFor = game.frame+rand(100);
                    }
                break;
            //Droid is going to hide in the hole
            case 1:
                this.frame--;
                //if Droid is hidden...
                if(this.frame<=0){
                    //Switch to Mode 2 (waiting)
                    this.mode=2;
                    //The next mode should be Mode 0 (appear)
                    this.nextMode=0;
```

```
                                //Set a random waiting time for 0 ~ 99 frames
                                this.waitFor = game.frame+rand(100);
                                //reset flag as the whacked Droid disappears
                                this.currentlyWhacked = false;

                                //Reduce maximum amount of Droids
                                maxDroid--;
                                //If the amount is exceeded the Droid should not appear
                                if(maxDroid<=0) {
                                    this.mode=3;
                                    if(maxDroid <= -1*totalDroid + 1) {
                                        game.end(scoreLabel.score, scoreLabel.text);
                                    }
                                }
                            }
                        }
                        break;
                    //Droid is waiting
                    case 2:
                        //if the game's current frame is greater than
                        //the set frame to wait for...
                        if(game.frame>this.waitFor){
                            //Make a transition to the next mode
                            this.mode = this.nextMode;
                        }
                        break;
                }
            },
            //Whack Droid
            hit:function(){
                //Do nothing if the Droid has already been whacked
                if(this.currentlyWhacked)return;
                //only when Droid has appeared at least half-way
                if(this.frame>=2){
                    //Set the flag so we know he's been whacked
                    this.currentlyWhacked = true;
                    //Droid after being whacked
                    this.frame=5;
                    //Switch to waiting mode
                    this.mode=2;
                    this.nextMode=1;
                    //Number of frames to wait is fixed at 10
                    this.waitFor = game.frame+10;
                    //Add score
                    scoreLabel.add(1);
                }
            }
        }
    });
```

```
//ScoreLabel class definition, extending Label class
ScoreLabel = Class.create(Label,{
    initialize:function(x,y){
        //Call the Label class constructor
        enchant.Label.call(this,"SCORE:0");
        this.x=x;
        this.y=y;
        this.score = 0;
    },
    //Adds points to the score
    add:function(pts){
        this.score+=pts;
        //Change the displayed score
        this.text="SCORE:"+this.score;
    }
});

//Initialization
window.onload = function(){
    game = new Game(320, 320);
    //Load Droid image
    game.preload('mogura.png');
    game.onload = function(){

        //Display ScoreLabel
        scoreLabel=new ScoreLabel(5,5);
        game.rootScene.addChild(scoreLabel);

        //Line up holes in a 4x4 matrix
        for(var y=0;y<4;y++){
            for(var x=0;x<4;x++){
                var pit = new Pit(x*48+20,y*48+20);
                game.rootScene.addChild(pit);
            }
        }
    }

    game.start();
};
```

You can find the source code for this change at code.9leap.net (http://code.9leap.net/codes/show/23778).

For the time being, our Whack-A-Droid game is complete. However, there are plenty of other ways to make a Whack-A-Mole type game. You can whack moving moles or add levels in which the speed of the moles and position of the holes varies, and of course you can fight other things than Droids or let them appear from something other than holes (such as gates). By changing the rules and the theme, an infinite number of variations are possible.

Now it's your turn. Let your creativity flow and try to create a masterpiece that's uniquely yours. When you've completed your game, try uploading it to http://9leap.net. If you encounter problems, see Chapter 1 for information about uploading games.

Conclusion

In this chapter we focused on the process of designing a game using enchant.js. We looked at the unbreakable rules of game design, reviewed the game development process, and even designed a fully working Whack-A-Mole game. In the next chapter we examine one of the most classic prototypes in gaming, the arcade shooter, and explain step-by-step how to create one of these games with enchant.js.

CHAPTER 6

■ ■ ■

Creating an Arcade Shooter

In Chapter 5, we looked at game design and created our very own Whack-A-Mole (or should I say Whack-A-Droid?) game. In this chapter, we look at another game, an arcade shooter game, that is more complex than Whack-A-Mole.

In the arcade shooter, we include several features that contribute to a fun game: background music, non-playable characters (like good guys and bad guys), explosions, scrolling backgrounds, and more. Bringing together all these elements requires careful planning with regard to game design because all the classes we create must interact with each other. For example, a bullet fired from a player's ship should cause enemies to disappear. In addition to covering how the arcade shooter is designed and coded, we introduce several new topics including indicators, levels, and rotation.

Summary List

1. Exploring the Game and Setting Up
2. Setting the Groundwork of the Game
3. Creating the Player's Ship
4. Creating the Shoot Class
5. Creating the PlayerShoot Class and Making the Ship Shoot
6. Creating Enemies
7. Creating the EnemyShoot Class and Making Enemies Shoot
8. Making Enemies Move in an Arc
9. Explosions
10. Adding a Scrolling Background
11. Adding a Life Gauge

Building the Arcade Shooter

Let's start with the simplest version of an arcade shooter we can make and then work our way up in complexity. The game we code in this section is a simple shooting game. When the player touches the screen, the ship moves to the location of the touch and shoots bullets across the screen as long as the user is touching it. Enemy ships appear on the opposite side of the screen and shoot at the player's ship. If the player's ship is hit, the game ends. Every time players eliminate an enemy ship, their score will increase. The goal of the game is to obtain the highest score possible before being hit.

In Chapter 5, our approach was to write a simple, short bit of code, and then improve on it as we continued in the development process, playing the game at each iteration. We do that here as well, but since an arcade shooter is more complex than Whack-A-Mole, there is a significantly longer set of steps.

Exploring the Game and Setting Up

If you play the game we are going to code before we begin coding, you'll have a better idea how the game works. Do the following to acquaint yourself with the game and set up the environment you'll be coding in:

1. Play the game at http://9leap.net/games/1034 a few times to get a feel for the game we'll be making. Take special note of how the enemies appear randomly and how difficult the game becomes when there are many enemy bullets on the screen. This game is popular on 9leap.net because of its replay value. The experience is different each time because of the randomly generated enemies.

2. Fork the template at http://code.9leap.net/codes/show/29839. This template contains the necessary image files you need.

Setting the Groundwork of the Game

As always, it's best to start with the simplest elements of a game first, and then add the more complex elements. Here, we set up the Core object, set the background, and create a score. Do the following to set this up:

1. Initialize the enchant.js library and create the Core entity by copying the code in Listing 6-1 into the blank template. Because of the complexity of this section, we label sections of code with comments so we can refer to them later in the chapter.

    Listing 6-1. Groundwork of the Arcade Shooter

    ```
    enchant();
    //Class Definitions

    window.onload = function() {
        game = new Core(320, 320);
        //Game Properties
        game.fps = 24;

        game.onload = function() {
        };

        game.start();
    };
    ```

2. Create a black background by typing the code in Listing 6-2 into the game.onload function. This specifies the backgroundColor of rootScene to be black.

    Listing 6-2. Creating a Black Background

    ```
    //In-Game Variables and Properties
    game.rootScene.backgroundColor = 'black';
    ```

The backgroundColor property of rootScene can accept names of all standard colors and hex values for colors (for example, #FF0000 for red).

3. Click Run. The screen should turn black.

4. Create a game variable for the player's score by adding the code in Listing 6-3 to the //Game Properties section. Later, we'll make this variable increase in value whenever enemies are hit by bullets from the player's ship.

    Listing 6-3. Creating a Score Variable

    ```
    game.score = 0;
    ```

5. Create a ScoreLabel and add it to rootScene by adding the code in Listing 6-4 to the //In-game Variables and Properties section. The (8,8) specifies the top-left corner of the label to be placed 8 pixels to the right and 8 pixels down from the top-left corner of the game. Later, we'll update the value of the ScoreLabel with the value of game.score every frame.

    Listing 6-4. Creating and Adding a Score Label to rootScene

    ```
    scoreLabel = new ScoreLabel(8, 8);
    game.rootScene.addChild(scoreLabel);
    ```

The ScoreLabel class is part of a plug-in called ui.enchant.js that is included in the download package on enchantjs.com. It was also included when you forked the project from code.9leap.net, if you did so earlier. If you did not, you'll need to make sure the line <script src='/static/enchant.js-latest/plugins/ui.enchant.js'> </script> is added to your index.html file before continuing.

6. Click Run. The ScoreLabel should appear at the top of the screen with the word "SCORE:".

If you encounter any problems with your code, you can find a fully working sample at http://code.9leap.net/codes/show/29841.

Creating the Player's Ship

The next step is to create the player's ship, which we will create as a class. Do the following to create it:

1. Create a class definition for the player by entering the code in Listing 6-5 to the //Class Definitions section. For a refresher, the enchant.Sprite declaration creates the new class as an extension of the Sprite class, which means all properties and methods of the Sprite class will work on the Player class as well. Everything in the initialize function will be run when a Player object is created.

    Listing 6-5. Player Class

    ```
    // Player class
    var Player = enchant.Class.create(enchant.Sprite, {
        initialize: function(x, y){

        }
    });
    ```

2. Preload graphic.png, which contains all the images used in this game, by adding the code in Listing 6-6 to the //Game Properties section. Figure 6-1 shows the graphic.

   Listing 6-6. Preloading Images

   ```
   game.preload('graphic.png');
   ```

   Figure 6-1. Graphic.png

3. Define the Player class as a 16x16 instance of the Sprite class and specify graphic.png as its image by entering the code in Listing 6-7 into the initialize function of the Player class.

   Listing 6-7. Specifying Size and Image

   ```
   enchant.Sprite.call(this, 16, 16);
   this.image = game.assets['graphic.png'];
   ```

4. Make the location of Player to be whatever was specified when it was created and set the frame by adding the code in Listing 6-8 directly under what you just added.

   Listing 6-8. Setting Location and Frame

   ```
   this.x = x;
   this.y = y;
   this.frame = 0;
   ```

5. Create a variable to keep track of when the screen is being touched by adding the code in Listing 6-9 to //Game Properties. This will set in the touch event listeners we'll create next, and will be used to determine if bullets should be fired from the ship later.

   Listing 6-9. Keeping Track of Touch

   ```
   game.touched = false;
   ```

6. Back in the initialize function, add an event listener to move the Player to Y position of the touch event when a touchstart event occurs by entering the code in Listing 6-10. When the touchstart event occurs, we also set the game.touched variable to true. Notice how we don't need to put a line break between player.y = e.y; and game.touched = true;. The semicolons delineate the commands.

   Listing 6-10. Adding the Touchstart Event Listener

   ```
   game.rootScene.addEventListener('touchstart',
           function(e){ player.y = e.y; game.touched = true; });
   ```

7. Below that, add event listeners for both touchend and touchmove events to take care of all possible interaction from the player by adding the code in Listing 6-11.

Listing 6-11. Additional Event Listeners

```
game.rootScene.addEventListener('touchend',
        function(e){ player.y = e.y; game.touched = false; });
game.rootScene.addEventListener('touchmove',
        function(e){ player.y = e.y; });
```

8. Create an instance of the Player class and add it to rootScene by entering the code in Listing 6-12 directly below what you just added, still inside the initialize function.

Listing 6-12. Adding Player to rootScene

```
game.rootScene.addChild(this);
```

9. Create an instance of Player by adding the code in Listing 6-13 to the //In-game Variables and Properties section. The instance of Player is automatically added to rootScene because of the last step.

Listing 6-13. Creating an Instance of Player

```
player = new Player(0, 152);
```

10. Click Run. The ship appears on the screen. If you click and hold, the ship will follow your cursor up and down on the screen.

If you encounter problems in this section, you can find a working code sample at http://code.9leap.net/codes/show/29845.

Creating the Shoot Class

There will be two types of ammunition in this game: the ammunition shot by the player's ship and the ammunition shot by enemies. Both types use the same image, so we'll start by creating a generic Shoot class. Do the following to create it:

1. Create the basic Shoot class by entering the code in Listing 6-14 beneath the //Player Class definition. It should have two functions: initialize and remove. It should also extend the Sprite class. When an instance of the Shoot class is created, we will pass three values to it: an X coordinate, a Y coordinate, and a direction.

Listing 6-14. Creating the Shoot Class

```
// Shoot class
var Shoot = enchant.Class.create(enchant.Sprite, {
    initialize: function(x, y, direction){
    },
    remove: function(){
    }
});
```

2. Create the Shoot class as a 16x16 instance of the Sprite class, and create and assign necessary variables by entering the code in Listing 6-15 into the initialize function of the Shoot class. We will use the moveSpeed variable next to control the speed of movement and allow for easy modification of ammunition speed later on.

Listing 6-15. Instance Variables of the Shoot Class

```
enchant.Sprite.call(this, 16, 16);
this.image = game.assets['graphic.png'];
this.x = x;
this.y = y;
this.frame = 1;
this.direction = direction;
this.moveSpeed = 10;
```

3. Create an enterframe event listener to control movement by entering the code in Listing 6-16 directly beneath this.movespeed = 10;. Code entered here will be run on instances of Shoot every frame.

Listing 6-16. Creating an enterframe Event Listener

```
this.addEventListener('enterframe', function(){
        });
```

We'll add code to this event listener in the next section.

Controlling Direction with Cos and Sin

We created the Shoot class to accept a direction, but we don't know yet what kind of value is passed to indicate direction. We also have an event listener to process movement, but we don't know yet how to process movement based off of a direction. How do we do this? With the functions cosine and sine, commonly abbreviated as cos and sin.

To understand these functions, you need to first understand direction in terms of the unit circle, as shown in Figure 6-2.

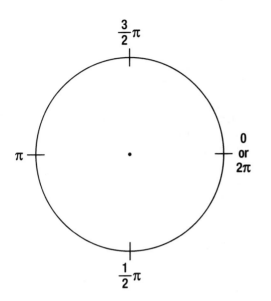

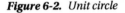

Figure 6-2. *Unit circle*

The unit circle specifies direction in terms of radians. One radian is equal to the length of the radius of a circle, lined up on its circumference. The pi symbol in the circle is a mathematical constant equal to a circle's circumference divided by its diameter (around 3.14). How is this relevant? Because cos and sin only accept values in radians, and the major directions, left and right, are equal to pi and 0 (or 2 * pi), respectively.

Let's say you want to draw a line with a length of 1 from the center of the circle. Cos and sin will give you the x and y coordinates respectively of the endpoint of that line, given a direction in terms of pi. For example, if we want to move to the right of the point by 1, we would pass pi to cos to find out how much we would have to move along the x-axis to get there (-1). We would also pass pi to sin to find out how much we would need to move along the y axis (0).

This is how movement is processed with code. We choose a direction based off pi, then use cos and sin to figure out how much to move a sprite by every frame.

4. Inside the event listener you just created, specify how instances of the Shoot class should move based off cos and sin by entering the code in Listing 6-17. Multiplying the results of the calculations by moveSpeed allows the ammunition to be manipulated in terms of speed later, if needed.

    Listing 6-17. Controlling Movement with Cos and Sin

    ```
    this.x += this.moveSpeed * Math.cos(this.direction);
    this.y += this.moveSpeed * Math.sin(this.direction);
    ```

5. Designate instances of the Shoot class to call the remove function if the shots stray far outside the bounds of the game screen by entering the code in Listing 6-18 inside the enterframe event listener, below what you just added. We could use 0 for the minimum allowed values of X and Y before the remove function is called, but using -this.width and -this.height ensures the shots don't disappear off the screen unnaturally. Do not worry about defining what the remove function does just yet.

Listing 6-18. Calling the remove Function

```
if(this.y > 320 || this.x > 320 || this.x < -this.width || this.y < -this.height){
        this.remove();
}
```

6. Inside the definition of the remove function, under the definition of the initialize function, specify what should happen when the remove function is called by entering the code in Listing 6-19. The delete command removes a given instance of the Shoot class from memory. In a very long game, if this is not specified it could bog down the system.

Listing 6-19. The remove Function

```
game.rootScene.removeChild(this);
delete this;
```

7. Add instances of the Shoot class to rootScene on creation by adding the code in Listing 6-20 to the initialize function, after the event listener.

Listing 6-20. Adding Shoot to rootScene

```
game.rootScene.addChild(this);
```

Creating the PlayerShoot Class and Making the Ship Shoot

We created the generic Shoot class, but now we need to create a class just for the ammunition shot by the player's ship, and create instances of it when the ship shoots. Do the following to create this class:

1. In the //Class Definitions section, create the PlayerShoot class and its initialize function by entering the code in Listing 6-21.

Listing 6-21. Creating the PlayerShoot Class

```
// PlayerShoot class
var PlayerShoot = enchant.Class.create(Shoot, { // Succeeds bullet class
    initialize: function(x, y){
        }
});
```

2. Create the PlayerShoot class as an instance of the Shoot class, specifying 0 as the direction, by inserting the code in Listing 6-22 into the initialize function. Remember the unit circle? The value of 0 is equal to a direction facing the right side of the screen. Because the ship is on the left side of the screen, bullets fired will head toward the right.

Listing 6-22. Creating an Instance of the Shoot Class

```
Shoot.call(this, x, y, 0);
```

3. We now need make the ship fire instances of the `PlayerShoot` class. Go back to the `Player` class definition and create an `enterframe` event listener inside the `initialize` function by entering the code in Listing 6-23 right above the line `game.rootScene.addChild(this);`.

    Listing 6-23. Enterframe Event Listener

    ```
    this.addEventListener('enterframe', function(){
    });
    ```

4. Inside this event listener, add the code in Listing 6-24 to create an `if` statement to be executed once every three frames and to be executed if the game is being touched.

    Listing 6-24. If Statement to Control Shots

    ```
    if(game.touched && game.frame % 3 === 0){
    }
    ```

5. Inside the `if` statement, create a new instance of the `PlayerShoot` class by entering the code in Listing 6-25.

    Listing 6-25. Creating an Instance of `PlayerShoot`

    ```
    var s = new PlayerShoot(this.x, this.y);
    ```

6. Click Run. When you click the screen, your ship shoots ammunition across the screen.

If you encounter problems in this section, you can find a fully working code sample at `http://code.9leap.net/codes/show/29907`.

Creating Enemies

Our ship can now shoot bullets, but now we need to create something for the ship to shoot at. Do the following to create a class for enemies and add them to the game:

1. Create the basic Enemy class definition with an `initialize` and `remove` function by adding the code in Listing 6-26 to the `//Class Definitions` section, below the `Player` class definition.

    Listing 6-26. Basic Enemy Class

    ```
    //Enemy class
    var Enemy = enchant.Class.create(enchant.Sprite, {
        initialize: function(x, y){
        },
        remove: function(){
        }
    });
    ```

2. Make the Enemy class a 16x16 instance of the Sprite class and assign the frame, x, and y variables by entering Listing 6-27 into the initialize function.

Listing 6-27. Making an Instance of Sprite and Assigning Variables

```
enchant.Sprite.call(this, 16, 16);
this.image = game.assets['graphic.png'];
this.x = x;
this.y = y;
this.frame = 3;
```

3. Specify the direction of movement for enemies to be to the left in terms of the unit circle (Math.PI), and create a variable for movement speed by entering the code in Listing 6-28 below what you just entered.

Listing 6-28. Creating Variables for Direction and Movement

```
this.direction = 0;
this.moveSpeed = 3;
```

4. Under what you just entered, create an event listener to move the enemy using the variables you just created by entering the code in Listing 6-29.

Listing 6-29. Moving Enemies

```
// Define enemy movement
this.addEventListener('enterframe', function(){
        this.x -= this.moveSpeed * Math.cos(this.direction);
        this.y += this.moveSpeed * Math.sin(this.direction);
});
```

5. Make the Enemy call the remove function (which we'll define soon) if it is outside the dimensions of the screen by entering the code in Listing 6-30 directly under the line this.y += this.moveSpeed * Math.sin(this.direction);.

Listing 6-30. Removing the Enemy if Outside the Screen

```
// Disappear when outside of screen
if(this.y > 320 || this.x > 320 || this.x < -this.width || this.y < -this.height){
        this.remove();
}
```

6. Finally, have the Enemy add itself to rootScene when it is created by entering the code in Listing 6-31 into the initialize function, under the event listener you just added.

Listing 6-31. Adding Enemy to rootScene

```
game.rootScene.addChild(this);
```

7. Define the remove function by entering Listing 6-32 into the remove function. This will remove the enemy from rootScene and delete it from memory. Also, it will remove the enemy from an array we're going to create to keep track of enemies. (Hence the delete enemies[this.key];, which will be explained soon.)

Listing 6-32. Remove Function

```
game.rootScene.removeChild(this);
delete enemies[this.key];
delete this;
```

8. In the `//In-Game Variables and Properties` section, create an array to keep track of enemies by entering the code in Listing 6-33.

Listing 6-33. Creating an Enemy Array

```
enemies = [];
```

9. Under the new array, create an `enterframe` event listener for the game to create enemies randomly by entering the code in Listing 6-34. We create a variable inside the Enemy called `enemy.key` and assign the game's current frame to it because this gives us something to keep track of the enemies with. If we do not do this, we would not be able to reference a specific enemy later on, which is needed when the enemies stray off screen or are hit with ammunition from the ship. Enemies have approximately a 1 in 10 chance of being created because of `if(Math.random()*100 < 10)` and, if created, are placed randomly on the y-axis.

Listing 6-34. Creating Enemies in the Game

```
game.rootScene.addEventListener('enterframe', function(){
    if(Math.random()*100 < 10){
        var y = Math.random() * 320;
        var enemy = new Enemy(320, y);
        enemy.key = game.frame;
        enemies[game.frame] = enemy;
    }
});
```

10. Update the game's `scoreLabel` every frame by entering the code in Listing 6-35 underneath the `if` statement, but still inside the event listener.

Listing 6-35. Updating the Game Score Every Frame

```
scoreLabel.score = game.score;
```

11. Hit Run. Enemies are created and fly across the screen. However, when the ship's bullets hit them, nothing happens.

12. Make the ship's ammunition destroy enemies with an event listener by entering the code in Listing 6-36 into the `PlayerShoot` class definition, under `Shoot.call(this, x, y, 0);`. The way this for loop is constructed causes the program to go through every single member of the enemies array, checking to see if the given bullet is in contact with it. If so, both the bullet and the enemy in the array are removed, and the player's score is increased by 100.

Listing 6-36. Making PlayerShoot Destroy Enemies

```
this.addEventListener('enterframe', function(){
    // Judges whether or not player's bullets have hit enemy
    for(var i in enemies){
        if(enemies[i].intersect(this)){
```

```
                    // Eliminates enemy if hit
                    this.remove();
                    enemies[i].remove();
                    //Adds to score
                    game.score += 100;
                }
            }
        });
```

13. Click Run. You now can take out enemies by shooting them. If you encounter problems in this section, you can find a working code sample at http://code.9leap.net/codes/show/29929.

Creating the enemyShoot Class and Making Enemies Shoot

At this point, there is no way to lose the game, which isn't very compelling. Let's create a class for enemy ammunition and make the enemies fire on the ship to increase the difficulty by doing the following:

1. Create the enemyShoot class by adding the code in Listing 6-37 in the //Class Definitions section. Create it as an instance of the Shoot class, with the direction set as Math.PI, as that faces left in the unit circle.

Listing 6-37. enemyShoot Class

```
// Class for enemy bullets
var EnemyShoot = enchant.Class.create(Shoot, { // Succeeds bullet class
    initialize: function(x, y){
        Shoot.call(this, x, y, Math.PI);
    }
});
```

2. Add an enterframe event listener inside the initialize function by adding the code in Listing 6-38 under the line that begins with Shoot.call. This event listener should contain an if statement specifying that the game should end if the center of player and the center of a given enemy bullet is 8 pixels or less at any given time.

Listing 6-38. Specifying Hits Between playerShoot and player

```
this.addEventListener('enterframe', function(){
    if(player.within(this, 8)){
        game.end(game.score, "SCORE: " + game.score);
    }
});
```

3. Make the Enemy class create instances of the enemyShoot class every 10 frames by changing the if statement inside the Enemy enterframe event listener to match what is shown in Listing 6-39. The variable age can be called on any Entity and gives the number of frames the Entity has been alive.

Listing 6-39. Making Enemies Shoot

```
// Disappear when outside of screen
if(this.y > 320 || this.x > 320 || this.x < -this.width || this.y < -this.height){
    this.remove();
}else if(this.age % 10 === 0){ // Fire every 10 frames
    var s = new EnemyShoot(this.x, this.y);
}
```

4. Hit Run. The enemies now shoot back.

If you encounter problems in this section, you can find a working code sample at http://code.9leap.net/codes/show/30105.

Making Enemies Move in an Arc

Enemies currently move in a straight line. This makes playing the game fairly straightforward, but a little simple. Let's make enemies move in an arc to make the game more interesting. We'll do this by creating a variable specifying if the direction should change in an upward motion or a downward motion (theta), depending on where the enemy gets created, and then change the direction slightly every frame. Do the following to make this happen:

1. Each enemy needs to have a variable that will be used to change its direction. Create a variable (theta) that is passed as an argument when an Enemy is created by changing the opening line of the initialize function to match the code in Listing 6-40.

Listing 6-40. Adding the theta Variable

```
initialize: function(x, y, theta){
```

2. Although direction is specified in terms of the unit circle, it's easier to work in degrees for specific amounts other than 0 or Math.PI. We'll be passing a value in degrees to theta, so convert it to radians by entering the code in Listing 6-41 right before the line that reads this.direction = 0;.

Listing 6-41. Converting theta to Radians

```
this.theta = theta * Math.PI / 180;
```

3. Inside the enterframe event listener of the Enemy class, make theta change the direction of the Enemy every frame by entering the code in Listing 6-42 directly under the line that reads this.addEventListener('enterframe', function(){.

Listing 6-42. Incrementing Enemy Direction

```
this.direction += this.theta;
```

4. Now enemies can accept a value for theta, and this will change the direction of the Enemy every frame, but we need to specify how the enemies are created to really use this. To accomplish this, change the if statement inside the game's rootScene enterframe event listener to match the code in Listing 6-43. If the Enemy is created in the upper half of the screen, the enemy will arc upwards (direction angle will increase by 1 each frame). If it is created in the lower half of the screen, it will arc downwards (direction angle will decrease by 1 each frame).

Listing 6-43. Creating Enemies that Arc

```
if(rand(100) < 10){
        // Make enemies appear randomly
        var y = rand(320);
        if (y < 160) {
                theta = 1;
        } else {
                theta = -1;
        }
        var enemy = new Enemy(320, y, theta);
        enemy.key = game.frame;
        enemies[game.frame] = enemy;
}
```

5. Click Run. Enemies move in an arc, making the game more compelling. Your game should appear as it does in Figure 6-3.

Figure 6-3. *Simple shooting game*

If you encounter problems in this section, you can find a working code sample at http://code.9leap.net/codes/show/30564.

Beefing Up the Game

Currently, our game in its current state is a working game. We could leave it here and move on to another game, but let's investigate a few ways to make the game more compelling by adding in some features.

We'll make several additions to the original game, and explain how to do so in the following sections.

Explosions

First, let's add some explosions. Currently, when enemy ships are shot down, they simply disappear. Let's add a bit of excitement by causing an explosion to appear when an enemy ship is hit.

1. Download the explosion (Figure 6-4) sprite sheet from
    http://enchantjs.com/assets/images/effect0.gif and add it to your project.
    We'll use this sprite sheet for our explosion.

Figure 6-4. *Explosion effect image*

2. Create a basic class, called Blast, as an extension of the Sprite class by adding the code in
    Listing 6-44 into the //Class Definitions section. The class should have an initialize
    and remove function.

    Listing 6-44. Blast Class

```
// Class for explosions
var Blast = enchant.Class.create(enchant.Sprite, {
    initialize: function(x, y){
    },
    remove: function(){
    }
});
```

3. Inside the initialize function, create the Blast class as a 16x16 instance of the Sprite
    class, and pass the x and y arguments to the local variables x and y by entering the code
    in Listing 6-45.

    Listing 6-45. Assigning Variables in Blast

```
enchant.Sprite.call(this,16,16);
this.x = x;
this.y = y;
```

4. Jump down to the window.onload function and add a preload statement under
    game.preload('graphic.png'); to add the sprite sheet of the explosion by entering
    the code in Listing 6-46.

    Listing 6-46. Preloading the Explosion Image

```
game.preload('effect0.gif');
```

5. Back in the initialize definition of the Blast class, under this.y = y;, add a statement
    to use effect0.gif as the image for the explosion by adding the code in Listing 6-47.

    Listing 6-47. Specifying effect0.gif as the Blast Image

```
this.image = game.assets['effect0.gif'];
```

6. Specify the frame to start at 0, and specify a duration of 20 frames by entering Listing 6-48 on the next line. We will use the duration soon to draw out the animation over a specific amount of time.

Listing 6-48. Specifying the Starting Frame and Duration

```
this.frame = 0;
this.duration = 20;
```

7. Below that, create an enterframe event listener by entering the code in Listing 6-49. We'll use this event listener to control the frame of the explosion.

Listing 6-49. Event Listener for Blast

```
this.addEventListener('enterframe', function(){
}
```

8. Inside the event listener, create a statement to set the frame of the explosion to go from 0 to 4 over a period of 20 frames by entering the code in Listing 6-50. This is accomplished with an algorithm. This algorithm first takes the current number of frames the explosion has been alive for (this.age) and divides it by the desired duration of the animation (this.duration) to get a fraction representing how far through the animation sequence the explosion should be. This is multiplied by 5 because the total sequence, shown in the sprite sheet, is 5 frames long. At this point, the result most likely has a decimal value (such as 4.42), so it is rounded down with Math.floor, and the result is what is assigned to the current frame of the explosion. The result is that the explosion progresses smoothly over 20 frames, and this value can be changed simply by editing the value of duration from 20 to something else.

Listing 6-50. Assigning a Value to frame

```
// Explosion animation
this.frame = Math.floor(this.age/this.duration * 5);
```

9. Beneath that, but still in the event listener, enter the code in Listing 6-51 to create an if statement that calls the remove function if the explosion has been alive for the desired duration. Note that if there is only one statement after the if statement, curly braces ({}) are not required.

Listing 6-51. Calling the remove Function

```
if(this.age == this.duration) this.remove();
```

10. Under the if statement, outside of the event listener, but still inside the initialize function, add the blast to rootScene by entering the code in Listing 6-52.

Listing 6-52. Adding Blast to rootScene

```
game.rootScene.addChild(this);
```

11. Make the remove function remove the blast from rootScene by entering the code in Listing 6-53 into the definition of the remove function.

Listing 6-53. Removing Blast from rootScene

```
game.rootScene.removeChild(this);
```

12. Make playerShoot create an instance of the Blast class if it hits an enemy by rewriting the definition of playerShoot to match the code in Listing 6-54. The line you should add is in bold type.

Listing 6-54. Making playerShoot create Instances of Blast

```
// PlayerShoot class
var PlayerShoot = enchant.Class.create(Shoot, { // Succeeds bullet class
    initialize: function(x, y){
        Shoot.call(this, x, y, 0);
        this.addEventListener('enterframe', function(){
                // Judges whether or not player's bullets have hit enemy
                for(var i in enemies){
                    if(enemies[i].intersect(this)){
                    //Start Explosion
                    var blast = new Blast(enemies[i].x,enemies[i].y);
                        // Eliminates enemy if hit
                        this.remove();
                        enemies[i].remove();
                        //Adds to score
                        game.score += 100;
                        }
            }
            });
    }
});
```

13. Click Run. Try playing the game and see how explosions appear when enemies are hit by bullets from the player's ship. If you did everything correctly, the game should appear as it does in Figure 6-5.

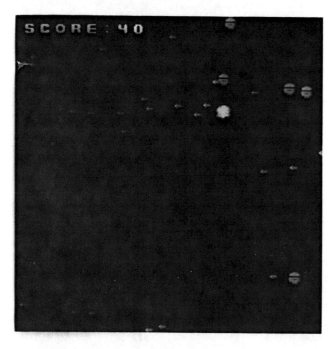

Figure 6-5. *Explosion-enabled arcade shooter*

If you encounter problems in this section, you can find a fully working code sample at
http://code.9leap.net/codes/show/30633.

Adding a Scrolling Background

Now that we've added explosions to the mix, things are starting to look a little better, but we've still got a ways to go. To add an element of quasi-realism, let's create a scrolling background for our game.

First, we need a background image exactly twice as wide as the screen. The left and right sides of the image should be exactly the same, with no stars being present on the extreme left or right. We'll see why in a moment.

We scroll this background image to the left one pixel at a time, and when we have arrived at the very end, we loop back to the beginning and repeat the process constantly throughout the game. This is why we want the left and right sides of the background image to be the same. It will look unnatural if players notice a sudden shift in the background. We'll use the image shown in Figure 6-6.

Figure 6-6. *bg.png*

By creating the Background class and adding in this loop motion, we create the illusion of an endlessly scrolling backdrop. Do the following to create the Background class and implement it:

14. In the //Class Definitions section, create a class for the background as an extension of the Sprite class by entering the code in Listing 6-55. The only method needed is the initialize method, as we never remove it from rootScene.

    Listing 6-55. Background Class

    ```
    // Background class
    var Background = enchant.Class.create(enchant.Sprite, {
        initialize: function(){
        }
    });
    ```

15. Inside the initialize function, create Background as a 640x320 Sprite by entering in Listing 6-56. This dimension is just as tall and twice as wide as the game screen.

    Listing 5-56. Creating as an Instance of Sprite

    ```
    enchant.Sprite.call(this,640,320);
    ```

16. Go to http://enchantjs.com/?p=731 and download the image file, bg.png, to be used as the background.

17. Upload the file to your project in code.9leap.net.

18. Inside the window.onload function, under the //Game Properties section, add Listing 6-57 to preload bg.png.

    Listing 6-57. Preloading the Background Image

    ```
    game.preload('bg.png');
    ```

19. Back inside the initialize function of the Background class, add Listing 6-58 to the variable declarations to position the background and assign bg.png to be used as the background image.

   Listing 6-58. Positioning and Image Variables

   ```
   this.x = 0;
   this.y = 0;
   this.image = game.assets['bg.png'];
   ```

20. Below that, but still inside the initialize function, add an enterframe event listener to move the background to the left by one pixel every frame by entering in the code in Listing 6-59.

   Listing 6-59. Moving Background Every Frame

   ```
   this.addEventListener('enterframe', function(){
           this.x--;
   });
   ```

21. Inside the event listener, underneath this.x--;, write a statement to reset the position of Background if it has been scrolled all the way over by entering the code in Listing 6-60. We know if the image has been scrolled all the way over if its x position is -320 or less.

   Listing 6-60. Resetting the Position of Background

   ```
   if(this.x<=-320) this.x=0;
   ```

22. Under the event listener, but still inside the initialize function, add Background to rootScene by entering the code in Listing 6-61.

   Listing 6-61. Adding Background to rootScene

   ```
   game.rootScene.addChild(this);
   ```

23. Finally, in the game.onload function, replace the line that reads game.rootScene.backgroundColor = 'black'; with the code in Listing 6-62 to create an instance of Background.

   Listing 6-62. Creating an Instance of Background

   ```
   background = new Background();
   ```

24. Click Run. The game should appear as it does in Figure 6-7.

Figure 6-7. *Arcade shooter with scrolling background*

If you encounter problems in this section, you can find a working code sample at
http://code.9leap.net/codes/show/30704.

Adding a Life Gauge

Currently, the player dies after just a single hit. It would seem much fairer if they went down after at least three hits. With that in mind, let's add something that gives the player multiple lives and allows them to withstand a few hits before dying. Do the following to make this happen:

1. In the game.onload function, under the //In-Game Variables and Properties section, add a variable as part of the Core object (game) to keep track of a player's life by entering the code in Listing 6-63.

    Listing 6-63. Creating a Lives Variable

    ```
    game.life = 3;
    ```

We've now initialized a variable representing the player's remaining number of lives. Because we do this inside game.onload and use game.life as the variable name (using the game. prefix to make it part of the Core object called game here), it can be referenced from anywhere inside the game.

2. Rewrite the EnemyShoot class to reduce the amount of life the player has by 1 if hit by an enemy bullet by making the class match the code in Listing 6-64. You should erase the line that reads game.end(game.score, "SCORE: " + game.score); and replace it with the code in bold type.

147

Listing 6-64. Reducing Life When Hit

```
// Class for enemy bullets
var EnemyShoot = enchant.Class.create(Shoot, { // Succeeds bullet class
    initialize: function(x, y){
        Shoot.call(this, x, y, Math.PI);
        this.addEventListener('enterframe', function(){
            if(player.within(this, 8)){      // Bullet has hit player
                game.life--;
            }
        });
    }
});
```

3. Under game.life--;, but still inside the if statement, write another if statement to end the game if the player's life is less than or equal to 0 by entering the code in Listing 6-65.

Listing 6-65. Ending the Game if No Life

```
if(game.life<=0)
game.end(game.score, "SCORE: " + game.score);
```

We've rewritten the game so that life is reduced by 1 when the player is hit, and if life hits 0 the game is over. We could create a class to display life, but there's not too much that needs to be added on the screen, so in this case it's more efficient to simply create the indicator within game.onload.

We'll be making the indicator with the MutableText class, provided as part of the ui.enchant.js plug-in. The MutableText class is very similar to the Label class, but instead of using fonts already installed in the computer to create text on the screen, it uses images of text characters from a sprite sheet, much like a Sprite.

■ **Note** The ScoreLabel class is an extension of the MutableText class and behaves similarly.

If we were to use the regular Label class here, the results would be pretty cheap looking because the system font will be used. By using MutableText, you can use a better looking font, and because of the use of an image instead of a system font, you can ensure the letters always look the same, regardless of what kind of browser or operating system the game is running on.

4. Within the game.onload function, below the line that reads player = new Player(0, 152);, create a new instance of MutableText by entering the code in bold type from Listing 6-66. The first argument (8), specifies the X position of the upper-left corner of the new instance, the second argument (320 – 32) specifies the Y position, the third (game.width) specifies the width of the label, and the fourth specifies the text that should be shown.

Listing 6-66. Creating the lifeLabel

```
game.onload = function() {
    //In-Game Variables and Properties
    background = new Background();
    game.life = 3;

    scoreLabel = new ScoreLabel(8, 8);
    game.rootScene.addChild(scoreLabel);
```

```
    player = new Player(0, 152);
    enemies = [];
    // Display life
    lifeLabel = new MutableText(8, 320 - 32, game.width, "");
```

5. Beneath the line that reads lifeLabel = new MutableText(8, 320 - 32, game.width, "");, but still inside the game.onload function, create an event listener to update the text of lifeLabel with a number of 0s equal to however many lives the player has left by entering the code in Listing 6-67.

Listing 6-67. Showing Number of Lives

```
lifeLabel.addEventListener('enterframe', function(){
    this.text = "LIFE " + "000000000".substring(0, game.life);
});
```

Because we define the text of the lifeLabel inside an enterframe event listener, the life gauge will be updated every frame.

Let's take a look at the "000000000".substring(0, game.life); part. This "0" stands for a single life in the game. "000000000" is a JavaScript character string object, so we can directly call up methods to be applied to that character string. We can extract text from the start of a string to a designated point by using the substring() method.

It should be noted that the second argument of the substring() method represents the point before which the substring should extract characters from. Remember that location references in strings and arrays begin with 0. This means that if game.life is equal to 3 and the substring is processed with "000000000".substring(0, game.life);, the substring will return the 0 in position 0, position 1, and position 2, but will stop before it reaches the third position.

This is why the game begins with three lives, represented by three 0s in the game ("LIFE 000"). As life diminishes, it will display "LIFE 00" and then "LIFE 0."

As you can see, enchant.js allows you to create game indicators easily without having to create an entirely new class.

6. Finally, under the event listener, add the lifeLabel to rootScene by entering in the code in Listing 6-68.

Listing 6-68. Adding lifeLabel to rootScene

```
game.rootScene.addChild(lifeLabel);
```

7. Click Run. The life meter will appear as it does in Figure 6-8.

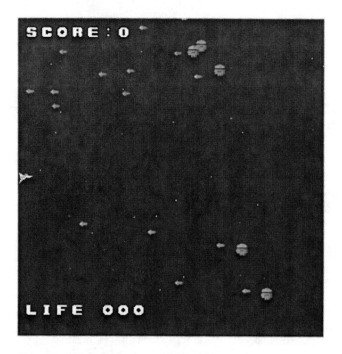

Figure 6-8. *Arcade shooter with life gauge*

If you encounter problems in this section, you can find a fully working code sample at
http://code.9leap.net/codes/show/30801.

Conclusion

Hopefully, you can see that the overall flow of the final shooting program is not so different from the simple prototypes
we looked at earlier in this chapter. In fact, the Background class and many other classes are exactly the same as in the
prototype we examined at the beginning of the chapter.

Just as we saw Chapter 5, in the Whack-A-Droid example, by rewriting and improving on a prototype bit by bit,
a full-fledged and complex game can be developed.

In this chapter, we explored the development of a shooting game, looking at how to create classes for bullets,
enemies, and the player, as well as how to deal with the collision detection between bullets and enemies or the player
ship. We then examined more advanced concepts that can be used to improve the basic game, including explosions,
a life gauge, and more.

In the next chapter, we'll look at creating standalone games outside of code.9leap.net, and investigate using
3D to create games with the gl.enchant.js plugin.

■ ■ ■

CHAPTER 7

Creating a Stand-Alone 3-D Game

The arcade shooter we created in Chapter 6 is an example of a two-dimensional game. Sprites, labels, and even the scenes in a standard enchant.js game exist on a flat plane, as seen by the existence of only an x and y axis within the game. Although we can stack entities on top of each other, this is simply to manipulate visibility. There is no "depth" that can be controlled.

Enchant.js comes with a plug-in called gl.enchant.js, which enables three-dimensional games to be created. In this chapter, we explore how to use gl.enchant.js to create a 3-D version of the Whack-A-Mole game we created earlier. On the way, we cover the essential topics of gl.enchant.js, namely 3-D Scenes, 3-D Cameras, and 3-D Sprites.

Before we get into 3-D games, however, let's take a second look at creating your own enchant.js games outside of code.9leap.net and briefly explore what is needed to put together an enchant.js game from scratch. At the time of the writing of this book, code.9leap.net supports most, but not all, functions of enchant.js plug-ins. We need to use one of these functions in our 3-D version of Whack-A-Mole.

Stand-Alone Games

Until now, practically all our code examples and instructions have recommended the use of code.9leap.net for simplicity. It is an easy way to keep track of your code and develop on-the-fly. That being said, to take your game development to the next level, it is important to understand how to put together an enchant.js game from scratch if ever the need arises.

There are a number of reasons you might need or want to create a stand-alone game. First, because code.9leap.net is in beta, certain file formats are not supported for upload into projects. Currently, 3-D model files cannot be uploaded into a code.9leap.net project. That is why when you make a 3D game, it cannot be written inside code.9leap.net. The other reason for creating a stand-alone game instead of a game hosted on code.9leap.net is to host it on your own web site.

Creating a game from scratch involves preparing all the files necessary for a game locally on your computer. While game authoring and testing can be done on standard local files (in other words, double-clicking on an index.html file to open it in a browser), some functions, such as loading 3-D data from a file, require the browser to have evidence the file is being accessed from a web server. This is due to a security restriction known as the *same origin policy*.

Same Origin Policy

The same origin policy is a security measure for restricting the ability of certain files to be loaded by a script. In enchant.js games, files usually affected by the policy are those containing sound or 3-D data. However, it's best to think of all files, except for images, as restricted by this policy. The same origin policy can be overridden by using specific commands or settings, depending on your browser.

Chrome

In Chrome, you can override the same origin policy by opening Chrome with a specific argument. Open up Terminal (Mac) or the command prompt (Windows) and type the following:

- *Mac*: `open /applications/Google\ Chrome.app --args --allow-file-access-from-files`

- *Windows*: `C:\Program Files\Chrome\Chrome.exe --allow-file-access-from-files`

Firefox

In Firefox, you can override the same origin policy through a setting:

1. Type `about:config` in the address bar. Click to accept the warning message if Firefox alerts you that changing these settings might affect the performance of the browser.

2. In the search box that appears under the address bar, type `origin`.

3. Double-click security.fileuri.strict_origin_policy to set the value to `false`.

Safari

Safari also supports disabling the same origin policy:

1. Go to Safari Preferences (Safari ➤ Preferences (Mac), File ➤ Preferences (Windows)), click the Advanced tab, and check the box that says Show Develop menu in menu bar.

2. Close the settings window, click the Develop menu, and choose Disable local file restrictions.

Internet Explorer

We highly recommend against developing games in Internet Explorer, as several features of HTML5 are not supported.

While disabling the same origin policy is a quick fix, we recommend installing a web server for larger development projects. This will help make the transition to the final release easier.

Local Web Servers

Local web servers allow files that make up a web site to be accessed in a way similar to how files are accessed off a standard server from the Internet. A variety of free server emulators are available online. An emulator is a virtual version of hardware. Instead of having a physical server running a web site, you can download and run a virtual server with emulation software. This makes working on web sites easier, as you do not need to upload your files to a server on the Internet to test it. We recommend XAMPP at `http://sourceforge.net/projects/xampp/` for Windows, Mac, or Linux or MAMP at `http://www.mamp.info/`, which is for Mac only. These emulators are free and easily available.

For this exercise we use XAMPP, but feel free to use any other web server if you are familiar with it.

Setup

To get started, download and install XAMPP from its project page on SourceForge, as shown in Figure 7-1.

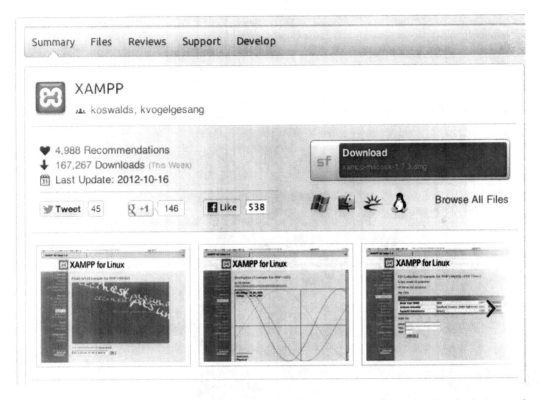

Figure 7-1. *The XAMPP official SourceForge project page (`http://sourceforge.net/projects/xampp/`)*

If you encounter any problems with installation, or if you would like to learn more technical details about XAMPP, you can find official documentation and installation instructions at `http://www.apachefriends.org/en/xampp-macosx.html` (for Mac) or `http://www.apachefriends.org/en/xampp-windows.html` (for Windows). Open XAMPP after installing it, and make sure the indicator light next to Apache is green or the Apache service has been started before continuing.

Once you have installed XAMPP (or another web server package) and it is currently running, navigate to the root folder of the web server. If you are using XAMPP on a Mac, you can access this at `/Applications/XAMPP/htdocs/` (Mac) or `C:\xampp\htdocs` (Windows). This is where you will put all your files for the game. If, for instance, you put a file called `index.html` into this `htdocs` folder, you'll be able to view it through a browser by visiting `http://localhost/index.html`.

3-D Games

While 2-D games are based on entities that move around on a flat space, 3-D games are based on depth. For the player, this means there is more to see and more aspects to see it from. The game space exists in three dimensions: length, width, and height (x, y, and z). This environment supports the viewing of objects within it from any angle. However, this means the game-creating process is more complex for the programmer.

While the benefits of a 3-D game include the possibility of creating a more immersive environment (in other words, making the player see through the eyes of a virtual character that can move and look around the game world), 3-D can also be used to create simple games enhanced with visual upgrades. Specifically, by altering the position of the camera during the game, you can create a level of depth that is visually impressive when compared to most games created in enchant.js.

You need to consider a larger number of variables when you create a game in three dimensions than a game in two dimensions. Many events that occur inside a 3-D game cannot be created using the same functions that would cause the same event to occur in a 2-D game. As such, there is a completely separate set of plug-ins that enable 3-D games to be created in enchant.js.

Creating a 3-D Whack-A-Droid Game

For our game-creating exercise in this chapter, we create a 3-D version of the Whack-A-Droid game we made earlier. To do this, we use gl.enchant.js and learn how to implement the various elements of a gl.enchant.js 3-D game, including 3-D scenes, 3-D cameras, and 3-D sprites. Figure 7-2 shows what the game looks like when it is complete.

Figure 7-2. Whack-A-Droid 3-D

We walk through the creation of this game step-by-step. Let's get started!

1. Go to http://enchantjs.com/?p=731 and download the WhackADroid3D-initial zip file for Chapter 7 and unzip it to the directory being used by your local web server. Another file, WhackADroid3D-Steps, is available on the page under the WhackADroid3D-initial zip file that includes the entire source code that is shown after each major step in this chapter. Steps corresponding to the named folders (in other words, Step 1 -> /Step1/) are marked on the code listings in this chapter.

2. Open index.html in a text editor and make sure the code matches the code in Listing 7-1.

Listing 7-1. index.html Containing Plug-in References

```html
<html>
<head>
<title>Whack-A-Mole 3D</title>
<meta http-equiv="cache-control" content="no-cache">
<meta http-equiv="content-type" content="text/html; charset=UTF-8">
<script type="text/javascript" src="lib/glMatrix-1.3.7.min.js"></script>
<script type="text/javascript" src="lib/enchant.js"></script>
<script type="text/javascript" src="lib/nineleap.enchant.js"></script>
<script type="text/javascript" src="lib/gl.enchant.js"></script>
<script type="text/javascript" src="lib/collada.gl.enchant.js"></script>
<script type="text/javascript" src="lib/primitive.gl.enchant.js"></script>
<script type="text/javascript" src="main.js"></script>
<style type="text/css">
    body {
        margin: 0;
    }
</style>
</head>

<body>
</body>

</html>
```

The following list shows the different plug-ins that are loaded, with explanations for each:

- *glMatrix-1.3.7.min.js*: An open-source JavaScript library that contains the mathematical computations necessary to perform various operations with gl.enchant.js.

- *nineleap.enchant.js*: The 9leap plug-in for enchant.js. We use it here for the game start and end screens.

- *gl.enchant.js*: The core WebGL-enabling plug-in for enchant.js.*

- *collada.gl.enchant.js*: Allows 3-D models in collada (.dae) format to be loaded into enchant.js games.

- *primitive.gl.enchant.js*: Contains several pre-made 3-D objects that can be used in 3-D games.

* WebGL is a JavaScript API (or interface) that allows elements in web pages, specifically canvas elements – which are parts of an HTML5 web page used to draw graphics – to communicate with a computer's graphics card to render those graphics with hardware acceleration. The enchant.js plug-in, which allows for the use of WebGL in enchant.js games, gl.enchant.js, comes with the enchant.js package, and is primarily used for making 3-D games with enchant.js.

If any of these plugins are missing, you'll run into problems with the game, so ensure they are all in the code before moving on.

Creating a Scene3D and Lights

Just as in regular enchant.js games, 3-D enchant.js games also require a scene within which everything occurs. However, these scenes are categorized as "Scene3D" to indicate their 3-D nature in the code. When you create a new Scene3D, you are telling enchant.js to initialize and create a three-dimensional space that will support the addition of objects into it.

1. Open main.js, which should be empty, and type in the code in Listing 7-2 to set up the basics of the game. Notice how there is nothing new here just yet.

    Listing 7-2. Framework of the 3-D Game

    ```
    enchant();
    var game;

    window.onload = function(){
        game = new Core(320, 320);
        game.fps = 60;

        game.onload = function(){
        };

        game.start();
    };
    ```

2. Inside the game.onload function, create a new Scene3D by typing in the code in Listing 7-3.

    Listing 7-3. Creating a Scene3D

    ```
    scene = new Scene3D();
    ```

The Scene3D creates a dimensional space, as shown in Figure 7-3.

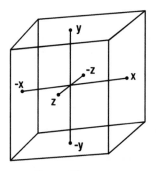

Scene 3D

Figure 7-3. Scene3D

Points within the 3-D space are designated on an x, y, and z axis, within a set of parentheses (x, y, z). If you look at the origin (x = 0, y = 0, z = 0) in the 3-D space from a point where x = 0, y = 0, and z = 10, the x axis would run left (-x) to right (+x), the y axis would run from down (-y) to up (+y), and the z axis would run from inside the screen (-z) to outside the screen, towards you (+z).

This is known as a right-handed system. If you stretch out your thumb and first two fingers in a way that each finger is at a 90-degree angle to the other two and imagine your thumb representing the x axis and your index finger as the y axis, your middle finger will form the z axis. Each finger represents the positive direction of each axis. In a left-handed system, the positive direction of the z axis would point away from you.

It is important to note that this coordinate system is different from how locations are determined in standard enchant.js 2-D games. In the normal 2-D environment, the top left-hand corner of the screen is designated as (0,0) and values increase to the right and below that point. In the 3-D system, the origin, or (0,0,0), is thought of as the center of the environment, as shown in Figure 7-3. Because of this, both positive and negative values are common.

3. Under the creation of the new Scene3d, but still inside the game.onload function, type in the code in Listing 7-4 to create a new directional light.

Listing 7-4. Creating a Directional Light

```
scene.setDirectionalLight(new DirectionalLight());
```

A directional light simply creates an array of light waves that bounce off of objects in the scene. Some of these light waves reflect off of objects and can be picked up by other objects, such as cameras, allowing them to be seen by the player. At the time of the writing of this book, directional lights created without parameters are created at a default point of (0.5, 0.5, 1). From this default point, a line is drawn to the origin of the scene (0, 0, 0). From the direction of this line, virtual light waves are generated that travel parallel to this line throughout the scene, as shown in Figure 7-4.

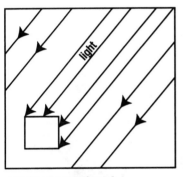

**2D Representation of
Directional Light Source
from Upper-Right**

Figure 7-4. *2-D representation of directional light source from the upper right*

We also could have created the directional light by writing (`var light = new DirectionalLight();` `scene.setDirectionalLight(light);`) instead of (`scene.setDirectionalLight(new DirectionalLight());`). If you use this var approach, you could change the origin of the light from its default position of (`0.5, 0.5, 1`) to another position with the properties `directionX`, `directionY`, and `directionZ`.

Creating a Camera3D

Although we now have our scene and a directional light, we still need a viewpoint from which to view the scene. If we have objects in a 3-D space, how the object looks will depend on where we're looking at it from. These viewpoints are designated as `Camera3D` objects in gl.enchant.js. They pick up the virtual light waves reflected off of objects in the scene from directional lights.

1. Create a Camera3D by typing in the code in Listing 7-5 under the creation of the DirectionalLight, but still inside game.onload.

    Listing 7-5. Creating a new Camera3D

```
camera = new Camera3D();
                        camera.y = 1.1;
                        camera.z = -1.65;
                        camera.centerZ = -10;
                        camera.upVectorZ = 10;
                        camera.upVectorY = 100;
```

Cameras have a default position of (0, 0, 10) when created, so with our additions in Figure 7-5, the camera is situated at (0, 1.1, -1.65). The camera object also has the properties centerX, centerY, and centerZ. These values specify a point at which the camera should "look at" or be pointed towards.

Figure 7-5. *Showing a Droid on the screen*

If a camera is located at one point and is pointed towards another point, the camera could rotate in any direction and still be pointed towards the specified coordinates. Think of it this way: if I am looking at you upside down, I am still looking at you. This is why there are "upVector" properties. These properties specify a point towards which the camera should consider as "up." By changing the upVector, the camera (and therefore the view of the camera) can be axially rotated.

You can place objects and cameras inside a 3-D space essentially at will. Multiple cameras can be created without any problems. As long as the camera is pointing towards the entities you create within the 3-D scene, you'll be able to see them. You might have to adjust your camera to get a more desired view of your objects, but the best way to achieve this is with practice.

Although we have now created the camera, specified where it should exist, what it should point at, and which direction is up, we still need to tell Scene3D to use it.

2. Make the scene use our new camera as the view for the player by typing the code in Listing 7-6 beneath camera.upVectorY = 100;, but still inside the game.onload function.

Listing 7-6. Designating the Scene's Camera

```
scene.setCamera(camera);
```

If there are multiple Camera3D objects inside the Scene3D, this function (setCamera) can be called at any time to switch between them.

Creating a Sprite3D

Sprites also exist in gl.enchant.js as Sprite3D objects and contain many similar properties and functions. In our game, we create multiple Droid characters, and each one will be an instance of Sprite3D. To save us from manually creating a new instance of Sprite3D each time we need another Droid, let's create a Droid class containing all the necessary variables and then call it whenever we need a Droid. Do the following to make this happen:

1. In the window.onload function, under game.fps=60;, add a line to preload droid.dae by typing in the code in Listing 7-7. This file was included in the download package earlier and is a 3-D model of the Droid image.

Listing 7-7. Preloading droid.dae

```
game.preload('images/droid.dae');
```

Files that end in .dae are in a format known as Collada. Collada is a file format for saving 3-D data and is supported by most major 3-D modeling software. Collada files can even be opened by Adobe Photoshop.

2. Above the window.onload function, create the Droid class as an extension of the Sprite3D class by typing in the code in Listing 7-8. The initialize function should include arguments for x, y, and z, which represent the position of the Droid on the x, y, and z axes respectively.

Listing 7-8. Creating the Droid Class

```
var Droid = Class.create(Sprite3D, {
    initialize: function(x, y, z) {
    }
});
```

3. Inside the initialize function, make Droid an instance of the Sprite3D class and set it to use the Collada file as its model by typing in the code in Listing 7-9. Notice how when working with Sprite3D, the image is not set through the image property, but rather through the set function.

Listing 7-9. Calling Sprite3D and Setting the Collada File

```
Sprite3D.call(this);
this.set(game.assets["images/droid.dae"]);
```

4. In its current form, the droid.dae file is too large, so scale it to 30 percent by typing in the code in Listing 7-10 on the next line.

Listing 7-10. Scaling Droids

```
this.scaleX = 0.3;
this.scaleY = 0.3;
this.scaleZ = 0.3;
```

5. Assign the arguments x, y, and z to their Sprite3D counterparts by typing in the code in Listing 7-11.

Listing 7-11. Assigning x, y, and z

```
this.x = x;
this.y = y;
this.z = z;
```

6. Inside the game.onload function, under the line scene.setCamera(camera);, add a new Droid to the Scene3D by typing in the code in Listing 7-12.

Listing 7-12. Adding a New Droid to Scene3D

```
scene.addChild(new Droid(0, 0, -8));
```

7. Save the file you are working on (main.js), but do not close it. If you are using a virtual web server, open up a web browser other than Internet Explorer and go to the path where index.html is stored (most likely http://localhost/index.html). Your screen should appear as it does in Figure 7-5.

If you encounter any problems with the code in this section, you can find a working code sample in the Step2 folder from the zip file mentioned earlier in this chapter.

We now have a legitimate, visible 3-D sprite, but to make it closer to a true game, we need to add some sort of interactivity.

Droid Interactivity

We need some sort of interactivity to make this a real game. Do the following to take the game to the next step:

1. Near the top of the code, under var game;, type in the code in Listing 7-13 to create a function to generate random numbers and some variables we'll use to keep track of the total number of Droids.

Listing 7-13. Creating a Random Number Function and Variables

```
function rand(n) {
    return Math.floor(Math.random() * n);
}
```

```
//Variables to keep track of droids
var maxDroid = 100;
var hitDroid = 0;
var combo = 1;
```

2. Below that, create a ScoreLabel by typing in the code in Listing 7-14. This ScoreLabel contains an add function to easily add and update the score.

Listing 7-14. Creating ScoreLabel

```
//Define ScoreLabel
var ScoreLabel = Class.create(Label, { //Extends Label class
    initialize: function(x, y) {
        enchant.Label.call(this, "SCORE:0"); //Call the Label class constructor
        this.x = x;
        this.y = y;
        this.score = 0;
        this.color = "#ffffff";
    },
    add: function(pts) { //Add the score
        this.score += pts;
        this.text = "SCORE:" + this.score; //Update display
    }
});
```

3. In the game.onload function, at the very end, create a new instance of ScoreLabel and add it to rootScene by typing in the code in Listing 7-15.

Listing 7-15. Creating and Adding ScoreLabel

```
//Display score label
scoreLabel = new ScoreLabel(5, 5);
game.rootScene.addChild(scoreLabel);
```

4. Edit the contents of the Droid class to match Listing 7-16. New code is in boldface. This will prepare the class for some interactivity upgrades in the next section, which will use the a and mode variables shown in the code sample. The tick function will be called every frame, and the hit function will be called whenever the player clicks on the Droid.

Listing 7-16. Restructured Droid Class

```
//Define Droid class
var Droid = Class.create(Sprite3D, { //Extend Sprite3D class
    initialize: function(x, y, z) {
        Sprite3D.call(this); //Call the Sprite3D constructor
        this.set(game.assets["images/droid.dae"]);

        this.scaleX = 0.3;
        this.scaleY = 0.3;
        this.scaleZ = 0.3;
        this.x = x;
        this.y = y;
        this.z = z;
        this.a = 0.01;
```

```
            this.addEventListener('enterframe', this.tick); //Define event listener
            this.addEventListener('touchstart', this.hit); //Define event listener for hit
            this.mode = 2; //Set initial Droid mode to wait, and then appear
            this.nextMode = 0;
            this.waitFor = game.rootScene.age + rand(100) + 75;
        },
        tick: function() { //Iterate Droid animation based on mode
        },

        hit: function() { //Hit Droid
        }
    });
```

Droid Appearance Behavior

In the Whack-A-Droid game, the Droids must behave in a specific way. First, they are created inside a hole until the game starts. Then, after a random amount of time, they appear from that hole. (For now, do not worry so much about the hole, but focus on the movement of the Droid.) They wait for another random amount of time, and then hide in the hole from which they first appeared. In our game, when they are outside their hole and are hit, they will fly up, off-screen, and a new Droid will appear in its place.

From this description, we can infer that a Droid will always be in one of five states at any given moment. Table 7-1 shows a listing of these states and the logic that drives that behavior. The mode number shown in the table is the number we will assign to the Droid when it is in that state to keep track of it.

Table 7-1. *States of a Droid*

State (mode number)	Description
Appearing (1)	Increase the y position of the Droid every frame until a certain point.
	Switch to Waiting mode with the intention to go to Hiding mode after a random amount of time.
Hiding (2)	Decrease the y position of the Droid every frame until a certain point.
	Switch to Waiting mode with the intention to go to Appearing mode after a random amount of time.
Waiting (3)	Once an allotted amount of time has passed, move on to the next mode.
Deactivated (4)	Do nothing. No more Droids should appear at this hole.
Flying Away (5)	Increase the y-position of the Droid every frame (at some point, the Droid will fly off the screen).
	After a random amount of time, reset the position of the Droid below the hole and set to Appearing mode.

These states will match up with a switch statement we'll create next in the Droid class declaration.

5. There is already an event listener that calls the tick function inside the Droid class definition. Type in the code in Listing 7-17 inside the tick function to create a system for moving the Droids.

Listing 7-17. The tick Function

```
if (game.rootScene.age === 0) {
    this.waitFor++;
}
switch (this.mode) {
    case 0: //Appear from hole
        this.a *= 0.98;
        this.y += this.a;
        if (this.y >= -1.2) {
            this.mode = 2;       //Go to wait mode after fully appearing
            this.nextMode = 1; //After wait mode, go to mode 1 (hide)
            this.waitFor = game.rootScene.age + rand(100) + 10;
        }
        break;
    case 1: //Hide in hole
        this.y -= this.a;
        this.a *= 0.98;
        if (this.y <= -1.5) {
            this.mode = 2;       //After fully hiding, go to wait mode
            this.nextMode = 0; //After waiting, go to mode 0 (appear)
            this.waitFor = game.rootScene.age + rand(100);
            //Reduce number of max droids (to control length of game)
            maxDroid--;
            //If number of max droids has been reached, and the given
            //Droid is instructed to hide, block the hole
            if (maxDroid <= 0) this.mode = 3;
        }
        break;
    case 2: //Wait
        if (this.y < -1.5) this.y += 0.05;
        if (game.rootScene.age > this.waitFor) {
            this.mode = this.nextMode;
            this.a = 0.05;
        }
        break;
    case 3: //Deactivated (no more Droids will appear from this hole)
        break;
    case 4: //Fly
        this.y += this.a;
        this.a *= 1.1;
        if (game.rootScene.age > this.waitFor) {
            this.nextMode = 0;
            this.waitFor = game.rootScene.age+rand(50) + 30;
            this.mode = 2;
            this.y = -3;
            this.a = 0.05;
        }
        break;
}
```

First, we tell the frame to wait for one frame before continuing to increase by one in the rare case that a Droid is created on frame 0 of the rootScene. This most likely wouldn't occur, but we want to cover our bases.

The a variable in the code is used for dynamic movement. During each frame, the value of a changes depending on which mode the Droid is in. For example, if the Droid is flying away, the value of a will increase by 10 percent (this.a *= 1.1;) every frame, and since the y position of the Droid is increased every frame by the value of a (this.y += this.a;), the Droid will fly up faster and faster as time elapses. This all happens very quickly, but adds a nice physics-simulating effect that appears more realistic.

Note that in case 4 (fly), after the waitFor value is reached by the game (in other words, after the Droid has flown off the screen), the Droid is repositioned back at (y = -3;), restarting the process and acting like a "new" Droid.

6. Define the hit function by entering Listing 7-18 into the hit function in the Droid class definition. This function is called whenever the player clicks a Droid.

Listing 7-18. The hit Function

```
if (this.y >= -1.4) { //If Droid is over halfway out of hole
    this.mode = 4;   //Enter fly mode
    this.a = 0.02;
    this.waitFor = game.rootScene.age + 30; //Wait for 30 frames (0.5s)
    scoreLabel.add(combo); //Add combo score
    combo++;
    hitDroid++;
} else {
    //If Droid is whacked before appearing out of hole, reset combo
    combo = 1;
}
```

If no Droid is hit by a player in the course of a game, the Droids will just loop through the Appearing, Waiting, and Hiding modes. However, this hit function, when called from the touchstart event listener earlier in the Droid class definition, will cause the following things to happen, line by line:

- If the droid is over half-way out of the hole:

    - Enter fly mode.

    - Set the modifier (a) to increase the y value (in fly mode) initially by 0.02.

    - Tell the droid to not change modes for 30 frames.

    - Add the user's current combo (starts at 1) to the overall score.

    - Increase the current combo by 1.

    - Increase the value of hitDroid by 1.

    - After 30 frames have elapsed, change the mode to 2 (Waiting), and reposition the Droid at (y = -3), from case 4 in the Droid definition.

- Otherwise (in other words, if the player tries to hit a Droid that isn't over halfway out of its hole):

    - Reset the player's current combo to 1.

Finally, we changed the position of the Droid we added to our Scene3D to (0, -1.5, -9.2). This wasn't completely necessary, but we did it to get a feel for how the Droid would look appearing and disappearing off of the screen.

7. Finally, reposition the Droid created and added to rootScene by replacing the line that reads scene.addChild(new Droid(0, 0, -8)); in the game.onload function with the line shown in Listing 7-19.

Listing 7-19. Adding a Droid With a Different Position

```
scene.addChild(new Droid(0, -1.5, -9.2));
```

We are changing the position of the Droid here because now that it moves around, it would not show up initially in the view of the camera otherwise.

8. Save the code and view the game in a browser. The Droid should pop up and down over time and should be clickable when it is in its up state. When the Droid is clicked, it should fly up the screen until it disappears, and another should take its place.

If you encounter problems in this section, you can find a working code sample in the Step3 folder of the download package.

Planes: The Signboards and More of gl.enchant.js

The enchant.js package includes the plug-in **primitive.gl.enchant.js**. This plug-in contains pre-defined objects of the most common 3-D shapes for use in your games. The object we'll be using in this section is a **plane**, which is simply a flat surface on which an image or color can be loaded. Because all these objects are built upon Sprite3D, any Sprite3D method or property is also useable or accessible to a plane. Do the following to implement planes in this game:

1. Change the game.preload('images/droid.dae'); line in the window.onload function to match what is shown in Listing 7-20. This is just loading in pictures to be used by the planes coming up.

Listing 7-20. Preloading Images

```
game.preload('images/pit.png', 'images/sign.png', 'images/droid.dae');
```

2. Create a Plane to represent the pit (containing the holes the Droids come out of) by typing in the code in Listing 7-21 after the line scene.setCamera(camera); in the game.onload function.

Listing 7-21. Creating the Pit

```
var pit = new PlaneXZ();
pit.scaleX = 3.0;
pit.scaleY = 3.0;
pit.scaleZ = 3.0;
var texture = new Texture(game.assets['images/pit.png'], { flipY: false });
texture.ambient = [1.0, 1.0, 1.0, 1.0];
pit.mesh.texture = texture;
pit.y = -1;
pit.z = -10;
scene.addChild(pit);
```

First, we create the pit variable as a new PlaneXZ. This is one of the predefined 3-D objects from primitive.gl.enchant.js. Since a plane is a 2-D object, it will exist only on two of the three 3-D axes, which is why we create the pit as a PlaneXZ. This designation tells enchant.js that the plane should be created in the two-dimensional space created by the X and Z axes.

Next, we scale the pit by a factor of 3 with scaleX, scaleY, and scaleZ. Planes are created using coordinates equal to -0.5 or 0.5 for each of their corners, or vertices (e.g., (-0.5, 0, -0.5), (0.5, 0, -0.5), etc.). By scaling these by a factor of three on all three axes, the final coordinates for the plane end up being either -1.5 or 1.5 for each value (e.g., (-1.5, 0, -1.5), (1.5, 0, -1.5), etc.). When you are creating your own games, you'll want to experiment with the scaling setting to see what looks best at your scene camera's angle.

The next step is to create a texture, which can eventually be applied to the plane you just created. Here, we load in pit.png as the image, and pass a parameter (flipY: false). Why do we do this? When applying textures to planes, enchant.js will do its best to figure out how to apply the texture in a way to make it appear right side up. However, sometimes enchant.js will get it wrong.

In WebGL, any object that can store pixels contains the property UNPACK_FLIP_Y_WEBGL, which flips an image along the vertical axis, and is assigned to the property flipY in gl.enchant.js. The flipY property defaults to true, so setting it to false in this way reverses the image along the Y axis. Although technically there is no Y axis on an XZ plane, a texture is two-dimensional, so the flipY designation will work as expected, as a texture has no Z axis. (If you're up for a challenge, you can find more information on how textures are handled in WebGL by searching for information on texture coordinates in OpenGL. WebGL is based on OpenGL.)

Moving on to the texture.ambient line, we set a value of [1.0, 1.0, 1.0, 1.0]. The first three values correspond to red, green, and blue, and the last value corresponds to the visibility or transparency of the light. A value of 1.0 is equal to 100 percent, so this translates to a white light with full visibility. The visibility value is used only in very specific instances, which will not be covered here.

Lastly, we apply the newly created texture to the pit's mesh texture property and adjust the position of the pit to place it somewhere appropriate on the screen. The final step is to add it to the Scene3D, and the pit will appear onscreen.

3. Directly under the line scene.addChild(pit);, type in the code in Listing 7-22 to create a red base for our pit. This adds a nice touch to the finished product.

Listing 7-22. Creating the Base

```
var base = new PlaneXY();
base.z = -8.6;
base.y = -2.5;
base.scaleX = 3.0;
base.scaleY = 3.0;
base.scaleZ = 3.0;
base.mesh.setBaseColor('#ff0000');
scene.addChild(base);
```

This code is pretty straightforward. We simply create the base as a new PlaneXY, position it, scale it, and then set a base color. Notice how the base color method accepts a hexadecimal value for the color. Any value valid for a CSS color property will be accepted here, but we like to use a hexadecimal value to keep things simple.

A value of #ff0000 translates to red, as the first two numbers correspond to red, the second two green, and the last two blue. Since the values are in hexadecimal, this value is in base sixteen. A value of ff corresponds to 256. Because only the red placeholder has a value, and the value is 256, the color of the base PlaneXY will be red.

Lastly we add base to the Scene3D to make it appear onscreen.

4. Beneath that, create a sign to make our game even snazzier by typing in the code in Listing 7-23.

Listing 7-23. Creating a Sign

```
var sign = new PlaneXY();
sign.scaleX = 2.0;
sign.scaleY = 2.0;
sign.scaleZ = 2.0;
var signTexture = new Texture(game.assets['images/sign.png']);
signTexture.ambient = [1.0, 1.0, 1.0, 1.0];
```

```
sign.mesh.texture = signTexture;
sign.y = 0.5;
sign.z = -8.6;
scene.addChild(sign);
```

There is nothing new here. Just like the pit, we create a new `Plane`, this time a `PlaneXY`, scale it, create a new texture (this time without the `false flipY` parameter as enchant.js positions the image correctly for our needs), set the ambient light for the texture, and assign it to the sign. After positioning the sign with the y and z properties, we add it to the scene.

5. Save the code and run it through a web browser. It should appear as it does in Figure 7-6.

Figure 7-6. *Whack-A-Droid 3-D with planes*

If you encounter problems, you can find a working code sample in the Step4 folder of the download package mentioned at the beginning of the chapter.

Replicating the Droid and Finishing the Game

We're now getting pretty close to having a finished game, but we still have only one Droid on our screen. Let's replicate that Droid to have a full collection, filling up our pit image.

1. In your code, create a Droid in each one of the holes shown in the pit by replacing `scene.addChild(new Droid(-1.1, -1.5, -9.2));` in the game.onload function with the code shown in Listing 7-24.

   Listing 7-24. Creating Multiple Droids

   ```
   //Create all Droids
   for (var j = 0; j < 3; j++) {
       for (var i = 0; i < 4; i++) {
           scene.addChild(new Droid(i * 0.75 - 1.1, -1.5, -9.2 - j * 0.9));
       }
   }
   ```

We created the Droid as a class that could be called and designated the behavior of all instances of that class, so replicating the Droid is as simple as using a for loop to iterate through all the ones we want to create.

The for loop controlled by the j variable represents each row, and the for loop controlled by the i variable represents each column in a given row. Notice how we multiply the x position by 0.75 in the new Droid declaration to move the space a new Droid will be created in over to the right. Similarly, we multiply the value of j by 0.9 before subtracting it from -9.2 to move the position of a new Droid back a row or two. It's a very efficient way to create multiple instances of anything in your enchant.js games.

2. Directly underneath this, type in the code in Listing 7-25 to create an event listener that ends the game once the maximum number of Droids has reached zero or lower.

   Listing 7-25. Ending the Game

   ```
   game.rootScene.addEventListener('enterframe', function() {
       if (maxDroid <= 0) {
           game.end(scoreLabel.score, "You whacked " + hitDroid + " Droids for a score of "
   + scoreLabel.score + " points!");
       }
   });
   ```

Because whacking Droids or allowing them to retreat back into their holes causes the variable maxDroid to decrement by one each time, we also add an enterframe event listener to end the game once maxDroid has reached 0 or lower, showing the number of droids whacked with the player's score.

▨ **Note**   Keep in mind that because the game.end function is fully supported only by the nineleap.enchant.js plug-in, the final message with a player's score and the number of Droids hit will appear only if the game is uploaded on 9leap.net.

---

3. Save the code and run it from a web browser. You should have a working game that appears as it does in Figure 7-7.

Figure 7-7. *After replicating the Droids*

If you encounter problems in this section, you can find a fully working code sample in the Step5 folder from the download package mentioned earlier in this chapter.

Panning Camera Effect

Although we have a working game now, let's add one final finishing touch: a panning camera effect at the beginning of the game. When the game starts, the player will have a bird's eye view of the pit, and then the camera will pan down to the view we've had up until now. This allows you to see the 3-D nature of the game you've just created.

Do the following to create the panning camera effect:

1. Inside the game.onload function, replace the lines that read camera.y = 1.1; and camera.z = -1.65; with the code in Listing 7-26 to change the initial camera position.

   Listing 7-26. Changing the Camera Position

   ```
   camera.y = 14;
   camera.z = -8.1;
   ```

This camera position is further away from the pit, but still angled towards it. This makes the panning effect more drastic and noticeable.

2. After the line that reads if (maxDroid <= 0) {game.end(scoreLabel.score, "You whacked " + hitDroid + " Droids for a score of " + scoreLabel.score + " points!");}, but still inside the event listener, type in the code in Listing 7-27 to make the camera pan down at the beginning of the game.

Listing 7-27. Making the Camera Pan at the Beginning

```
//Pan camera down at beginning
if (game.rootScene.age < 130) {
    camera.z += 0.05;
    camera.y -= 0.1;
}
```

The actual panning effect takes place here. For the first 130 frames of the game, the camera will get closer and closer to the pit, stopping at the perfect viewpoint. This is accomplished by modifying the z and y axis positions by a very small amount every frame to reach a specific point by the time 130 frames have passed. When developing something like this, it helps to calculate where you want the camera to start from, where you want it to end, and then figure out how much the camera needs to move each frame to achieve this.

3. Save the code and run the game through a web browser. The game should start from the viewpoint shown in Figure 7-8 and quickly pan down to the view that is featured in preceding code samples.

Figure 7-8. *Whack-A-Droid 3-D with a new starting perspective*

170

If you encounter problems in this section, you can find a working code sample in the Step6 folder available from the zip file mentioned earlier in the chapter.

Conclusion

In this final chapter, we took a look at how to develop a stand-alone 3-D enchant.js game. We briefly touched on WebGL and the various WebGL-enabled plug-ins of enchant.js: gl.enchant.js, primitive.gl.enchant.js, and collada.gl.enchant.js.

We created a 3-D version of our Whack-A-Droid game and saw how instances of Scene3D, Camera3D, and Sprite3D can be used to construct a 3-D environment and interface a player with it. By creating instances of planes and our self-authored Droid class, we were able to put together a working 3-D version of our Whack-A-Droid game, even adding a swooping camera effect at the end to show off the 3-D nature of our game.

We hope this chapter inspires you to experiment with 3-D on your own through enchant.js and eventually try authoring your own 3-D game. As 9leap.net supports any game created with enchant.js, we encourage you to publish your game on 9leap and share it with the world!

Stay connected with us:

- *Official site*: enchantjs.com

- *Reddit*: reddit.com/r/enchantjs – ask questions here!

- *Facebook page*: facebook.com/enchantjs

- *Twitter*: @enchantjs_en

- *GitHub*: github.com/wise9/enchant.js

Best of luck with your game authoring!
The enchant.js team

APPENDIX A

■ ■ ■

Class Appendix

This appendix contains information on the most common classes in enchant.js. Classes are first listed by which part of enchant.js they originate from (core library or plug-in), and are then organized alphabetically. Each class page contains a brief description on the overall function of the class, lists the classes that properties and methods are inherited from, provides the most common properties and methods for that class, and, for some classes, includes an example on how to use the class.

Classes are organized in a hierarchy and inherit methods and properties from their parent classes. The classes from which properties and methods are inherited are listed in the Inheritance section of each class listing and are shown in the form of a series of classes. The highest level parent class is shown at the left, and the listed class is shown on the right. For example, the inheritance tree for the Label class is as follows:

`EventTarget-Node-Entity-Label`

Therefore, in addition to being able to use all the properties and methods specified in the `Label` class, objects created as labels will be able to use all applicable methods from `Entity`, `Node`, and `EventTarget`. The `addEventListener` method (from `EventTarget`) could be run on a label, and the age property (from `Node`) could also be called on a `Label`.

For a complete list of classes in enchant.js, please refer to the official API under the reference section at `http://enchantjs.com`.

Appendix Contents:

1. Core Classes

    a. Core

    b. EventTarget

    c. Game

    d. Group

    e. Label

    f. Map

    g. Node

    h. Scene

    i. Sound

    j. Sprite

2. gl.enchant.js

   a. AmbientLight

   b. Camera3D

   c. DirectionalLight

   d. Light3D

   e. Scene3D

   f. Sprite3D

3. ui.enchant.js

   a. APad

   b. Button

   c. LifeLabel

   d. MutableText

   e. Pad

   f. ScoreLabel

Core Classes

Core classes are contained within the main enchant.js file. Nothing needs to be added to a set of files other than the basic library (enchant.js) to access core classes.

Core

The Core class is the main game container. The entirety of a game must reside inside a Core object. Only one can exist at a time, and if another is created, the original will be deactivated.

The Core class is also responsible for managing the Scene objects within a game. Changing the active scene, removing a scene, and adding a Scene are all part of objects of the Core class.

Extends

EventTarget
↳ Core

Common Properties

- assets: Objects for storing preloaded images.

- currentScene: The currently displayed scene.

- fps: The frame rate of the game.

- frame: The current number of frames that have elapsed since the Core object was created.

- height: The height of the game screen.

- `loadingScene`: A scene that gets displayed while the game loads.
- `rootScene`: The default scene of a game.
- `width`: The width of the game screen.

Common Methods

All examples assume a variable, game, has been created as an instance of the Core class.

Method	Explanation	Example
`popScene();`	Ends the current scene and makes the underlying Scene active.	`game.popScene();`
`preload(assets);`	Preloads an image or sound file to be used later in the game.	`game.preload("img/chara1.jpg");`
`pushScene(scene);`	Pushes a scene to the top of the scene stack, making it the active scene.	`game.pushScene(Scene3);`
`removeScene(scene);`	Removes a scene from the scene stack.	`game.removeScene(Scene2);`
`replaceScene(scene);`	Replaces the current scene with the designated one.	`game.replaceScene(Scene4);`
`start();`	Starts the game.	`game.start();`

Example

```
var game = new Core(320,320);
```

Entity

The `Entity` class contains objects displayed as DOM elements, or elements created as objects within a webpage. This class is not used directly (i.e., you never specify `var bear = new Entity();`), but contains a collection of properties and methods common to most visual elements in enchant.js. Because most visual elements (`Sprite, Label,` etc.) are children of the `Entity` class, visual elements also have access to these properties and methods.

Extends

`EventTarget-Node-Entity`

Common Properties

- `backgroundColor`: Specifies the color of the background. Color should be specified in any format valid for the CSS color property. (e.g., #ffffff, red, etc.)
- `buttonMode`: Designates this `Entity` as a button. When the `Entity` is subsequently clicked, the corresponding button event is dispatched. Valid values include left, right, up, down, a, and b.
- `buttonPressed`: Set as `true` if this `Entity` is being clicked. This only works if a `buttonMode` has been set.

- `height`: The height of the `Entity` in pixels.

- `opacity`: The opacity of the `Entity`. This is measured from 0 (completely transparent) to 1 (completely opaque).

- `originX`: The X position of the point of origin used for rotation and scaling.

- `origin`: The Y position of the point of origin used for rotation and scaling.

- `rotation`: Rotation angle of the `Entity` (in degrees).

- `visible`: Indicates whether or not the `Entity` is displayed. Defaults to `true`. Note that an `Entity` must still be added as the child of a `Scene` to show up on the screen.

Common Methods

All examples assume a variable, game, has been created as an instance of the `Sprite` class, which extends the `Entity` class. This is because an `Entity` cannot be created in and of itself.

Method	Explanation	Example
`intersect(Entity);`	Returns `true` if the `Entity` is touching or intersecting the specified `Entity`.	`bear.intersect(ball);`
`rotate(degree);`	Rotates the `Entity` by the number of degrees specified.	`bear.rotate(15);`
`scale(x,y);`	Scales the `Entity` in the x and y directions by the factors specified.	`bear.scale(2,2);` (scales the bear by 200%)
`within(Entity, distance);`	Returns `true` if the center point of the `Entity` is within the specified distance (in pixels) of the specified `Entity`'s center point.	`bear.within(ball, 50);`

Event

Events are not created directly by the developer, but are issued usually by a Core, Scene, or Node object. Using an `EventListener`, these events can be listened for, and then designated code can be executed when the event occurs.

Extends

Events are defined at the highest level in enchant.js and do not inherit from any class.

Common Events

Note that the "A" and "B" buttons described in the following table refer to virtual buttons created as part of the Button class from ui.enchant.js and designated to be "A" and "B" buttons. For more information, please see the entry for the Button class in the ui.enchant.js section near the end of this appendix.

Event type	Description	Objects issued
Event.A_BUTTON_DOWN	Event occurring when the "A" button is pressed	Core, Scene
Event.A_BUTTON_UP	Event occurring when the "A" button is released	Core, Scene
Event.ADDED	Event occurring when a Node is added to a Group	Node
Event.ADDED_TO_SCENE	Event occurring when a Node is added to a Scene	Node
Event.B_BUTTON_DOWN	Event occurring when the "B" button is pressed	Core, Scene
Event.B_BUTTON_UP	Event occurring when the "B" button is released	Core, Scene
Event.DOWN_BUTTON_DOWN	Event occurring when the down button is pressed	Core, Scene
Event.DOWN_BUTTON_UP	Event occurring when the down button is released	Core, Scene
Event.ENTER	Event occurring when a Scene begins	Scene
Event.ENTER_FRAME	Event occurring when a new frame is being processed	Core, Scene
Event.EXIT	Event occurring when the Scene ends	Scene
Event.EXIT_FRAME	Event occurring when frame processing is about to end	Core
Event.INPUT_CHANGE	Event occurring when a button input changes	Core, Scene
Event.INPUT_END	Event occurring when a button input ends	Core, Scene
Event.INPUT_START	Event occurring when a button input begins	Core, Scene
Event.LEFT_BUTTON_DOWN	Event occurring when the left button is pressed	Core, Scene
Event.LEFT_BUTTON_UP	Event occurring when the left button is released	Core, Scene
Event.LOAD	Event dispatched upon completion of game loading	Core
Event.PROGRESS	Events occurring during game loading	Core
Event.REMOVED	Event occurring when a Node is removed from a Group	Node
Event.REMOVED_FROM_SCENE	Event occurring when a Node is removed from a Scene	Node
Event.RENDER	Event occurring when an Entity is rendered	Entity
Event.RIGHT_BUTTON_DOWN	Event occurring when the right button is pressed	Core, Scene
Event.RIGHT_BUTTON_UP	Event occurring when the right button is released	Core, Scene
Event.TOUCH_END	Event occurring when a touch related to the Node has ended	Node
Event.TOUCH_MOVE	Event occurring when a touch related to the Node has moved	Node
Event.TOUCH_START	Event occurring when a touch related to the Node has begun	Node
Event.UP_BUTTON_DOWN	Event occurring when the up button is pressed	Core, Scene
Event.UP_BUTTON_UP	Event occurring when the up button is released	Core, Scene

Game

The Game object was rebranded as the Core object in version 0.6. Please see the Core object entry. Versions of enchant.js newer than 0.6 are backward compatible with the Game object, but as the Game object is obsolete, we strongly recommend using the Core object.

Group

The Group class is used to link together multiple Node objects for the purpose of either moving them as a single unit or operating on them in another way as a unit. Because all visible entities in enchant.js are of the Entity class, which extends the Node class, all visible entities can be added to a Group object.

Extends

EventTarget-Node-Group

Common Properties

- childNodes: An array of objects containing all nodes that are a member of the Group.
- firstChild: The first Node in the Group.
- lastChild: The last Node in the Group.

Common Methods

All examples assume a variable, set, has been created as an instance of the Group class. Because Group extends the Node class, any method that is valid for a Node will work on a Group object. (e.g., moveTo, moveBy, etc.)

Method	Explanation	Sample
addChild(node);	Adds a Node to the end of the Group.	set.addChild(bear);
insertBefore(node, reference);	Inserts a Node into a Group, before the reference position in the array of Node objects.	set.insertBefore(bear,3);
removeChild(node);	Removes a Node from the Group.	set.removeChild(bear);

Example Use

```
var stage = new Group();
stage.addChild(player);
stage.addChild(enemy);
stage.addChild(map);
stage.addEventListener('enterframe', function() {
   // Moves the entire frame based on the player's x coordinate.
   if (this.x > 64 - player.x) {
       this.x = 64 - player.x;
   }
});
```

Label

Labels are used to display text within the game.

Extends

EventTarget-Node-Entity-Label

Common Properties

- color: The color of the text in the Label. Color should be specified in any format valid for the CSS color property. (e.g., #ffffff, red, etc.)

- font: The font of the text in the Label. Font should be specified in any format valid for the CSS font property. (e.g., 16px serif; 12px sans-serif; etc.)

- text: The text to be displayed by the Label.

- textAlign: The horizontal alignment of the text. Alignment should be specified in any format valid for the CSS text-align property. (e.g., left, right, center, etc.)

Common Methods

There are no common methods for a Label other than the ones inherited from Entity, Node, and EventTarget.

Example Use

```
var title = new Label();
title.color = "blue";
title.font = "16px serif";
score.text = "Example Title";

game.rootScene.addChild(title);
```

Map

Maps are used to create maps from tilesets and display them.

Extends

EventTarget-Node-Entity-Map

Common Properties

- collisionData: Two-dimensional array specifying if collisions should be detected on specific tiles in the Map.

- image: The tile set image used for tiles in the Map.

- tileHeight: The height of tiles used in the Map.

- tileWidth: The width of tiles used in the Map.

Common Methods

All examples assume a variable, map1, has been created as an instance of the Map class.

Method	Explanation	Example
checkTile(x, y);	Checks to see what tile is present at a given position.	map1.checkTile(50, 50);
hitTest(x, y);	Returns true if the point specified is designated as containing an obstacle in the collisionData array.	map1.hitTest(50, 50);
loadData(data);	Sets tiles in the map from the tile set image.	map1.loadData(array);

Example Use

```
var map = new Map(16, 16);
map.image = game.assets['http://enchantjs.com/assets/images/map0.gif'];
map.loadData([
    [0,0,0,0,0,0,0,0,0,0,0,0,0,0,0,0,0,0,0,0,0,0,0,0],
    [0,2,2,2,2,0,0,0,0,0,0,0,0,0,0,0,0,0,2,2,2,2,0],
    [0,2,2,2,2,0,0,2,2,2,2,2,2,2,2,0,0,0,2,2,2,2,0],
    [0,2,2,2,2,0,0,2,2,2,2,2,2,2,2,0,0,0,2,2,2,2,0],
    [0,0,2,2,0,0,0,2,2,0,0,0,0,2,2,0,0,0,0,2,2,0,0],
    [0,0,2,2,0,0,0,2,2,0,0,0,0,2,2,0,0,0,0,2,2,0,0],
    [0,0,2,2,0,0,0,2,2,0,0,0,0,0,0,0,0,2,2,2,2,0,0],
    [0,0,2,2,2,2,2,2,2,2,2,2,2,2,0,0,0,2,2,2,2,0,0],
    [0,0,2,2,2,2,2,2,2,2,2,2,2,2,0,0,0,2,2,0,0,0,0],
    [0,0,0,0,0,2,2,0,0,0,0,0,2,2,2,2,2,2,2,0,0,0,0],
    [0,0,0,0,0,2,2,0,0,0,0,0,2,2,2,2,2,2,2,0,0,0,0],
    [0,0,0,2,2,2,2,0,0,0,0,0,2,2,0,0,0,0,0,0,0,0,0],
    [0,0,2,2,2,2,2,0,0,0,0,0,2,2,2,2,2,2,2,2,2,0,0],
    [0,0,2,2,2,2,0,0,0,0,0,0,0,2,2,2,2,2,2,2,2,2,0,0],
    [0,0,2,2,2,2,0,0,0,0,0,0,0,0,0,0,0,0,0,2,2,0,0],
    [0,0,0,2,2,0,0,0,0,0,0,0,0,0,0,0,0,0,0,2,2,0,0],
    [0,0,0,2,2,0,0,0,0,0,0,0,0,0,0,0,0,0,0,2,2,2,2,0],
    [0,0,0,2,2,2,2,2,2,2,2,2,2,2,2,2,0,0,2,2,2,2,0],
    [0,0,0,2,2,2,2,2,2,2,2,2,2,2,2,2,0,0,2,2,2,2,0],
    [0,0,0,0,0,0,0,0,0,0,0,0,0,0,0,0,0,0,0,0,0,0,0]
]);
```

Node

The Node class is for objects in enchant.js that are displayed through the display tree. Instances of the Node class are not directly created by the developer.

Extends

EventTarget-Node

Common Properties

- age: The number of frames the Node object has been alive.

- scene: The Scene to which the Node belongs.

- x: The x position of the Node object.

- y: The y position of the Node object.

Common Methods

All examples assume a variable, bear, has been created as an instance of the Sprite class, which extends the Entity class, which extends the Node class.

Method	Explanation	Example
moveBy(x, y);	Moves the Node object by the amounts specified (in pixels) on the x and y axes.	bear.moveBy(50, 50);
moveTo(x, y);	Moves the Node object to the location specified on the x and y axes.	bear.moveTo(60, 60);

Scene

The root of the display object tree. All Entity objects must be added to a Scene object to be visible.

Extends

EventTarget-Node-Group-Scene

Common Properties

There are no common properties for a Scene other than the ones inherited from EventTarget, Node, and Group.

Common Methods

There are no common methods for a Scene other than the ones inherited from EventTarget, Node, and Group.

Example Use

```
var scene = new Scene();
scene.addChild(player);
scene.addChild(enemy);

core.pushScene(scene);
```

Sprite

Sprites are for displaying images, usually of characters or game elements, in a game.

Extends

EventTarget-Node-Entity-Sprite

Common Properties

- frame: Index numbers of the frames to be displayed.
- height: The height of the Sprite in pixels.
- image: The image (sprite-sheet) from which a frame is pulled to represent the Sprite on-screen.
- width: The width of the Sprite in pixels.

Common Methods

There are no common properties for a Scene other than the ones inherited from EventTarget, Node, and Entity.

Example Use

```
var bear = new Sprite(16,16);
sprite.image = game.assets("img/chara1.gif");
sprite.frame = [0, 1, 0, 2];
        //shows frame 0, 1, 0, and 2 in sequence, incrementing up one each frame
game.rootScene.addChild(bear);
```

gl.enchant.js

This plug-in extends WebGL support to enchant.js, allowing for games in 3-D to be created.

AmbientLight

The AmbientLight class represents a light that generates light in all directions from the origin point of the light.

Extends

EventTarget-Light3D-AmbientLight

Common Properties

There are no common properties for AmbientLight other than the ones inherited from EventTarget, Node, and Entity.

Common Methods

There are no common properties for AmbientLight other than the ones inherited from EventTarget and Light3D.

Example Use

```
var scene = new Scene3D();
var light = new AmbientLight();
light.color = [1.0, 1.0, 0.0];

scene.setAmbientLight(light);
```

Camera3D

The Camera3D class creates a view from which a player can see inside of a Scene3D.

Extends

This class is defined in the highest level of gl.enchant.js. It has no parent class.

Common Properties

- centerX: The point on the X axis the camera is pointing toward.

- centerY: The point on the Y axis the camera is pointing toward.

- centerZ: The point on the Z axis the camera is pointing toward.

- upVectorX: The point on the X axis toward which the camera considers "up."

- upVectorY: The point on the Y axis toward which the camera considers "up."

- upVectorZ: The point on the Z axis toward which the camera considers "up."

- x: The location of the camera on the X axis.

- y: The location of the camera on the Y axis.

- z: The location of the camera on the Z axis.

Common Methods

All examples assume a variable, camera, has been created as an instance of the Camera3D class.

Method	Explanation	Example
altitude(amount);	Moves the Camera3D along the Y axis.	camera.altitude(2);
forward(amount);	Moves the Camera3D along the Z axis.	camera.forward(2);
lookAt(sprite);	Points the Camera3D towards a Sprite3D in the Scene3D.	camera.lookAt(droid);
rotatePitch(degrees);	Rotates the Camera3D along the X axis.	camera.rotatePitch(15);
rotateRoll(degrees);	Rotates the Camera3D along the Z axis.	camera.rotateRoll(15);
rotateYaw(degrees);	Rotates the Camera3D along the Y axis.	camera.rotateYaw(15);
sidestep(amount);	Moves the camera along the X axis.	camera.sidestep(2);

Example Use

```
camera = new Camera3D();
camera.y = 1.1;
camera.z = -1.65;
camera.centerZ = -10;
camera.upVectorZ = 10;

camera.upVectorY = 100;
```

DirectionalLight

The DirectionalLight class represents a light which casts light in one direction instead of in all directions.

Extends

```
EventTarget-Light3D-DirectionalLight
```

Common Properties

- directionX: The X position of the point towards which the DirectionalLight casts light.

- directionY: The Y position of the point towards which the DirectionalLight casts light.

- directionZ: The Z position of the point towards which the DirectionalLight casts light.

Common Methods

There are no common methods for DirectionalLight other than the ones inherited from EventTarget and Light3D.

Example Use

```
var scene = new Scene3D();
var light = new DirectionalLight();
light.color = [1.0, 1.0, 0.0];
light.directionY = 10;
light.directionX = 4;
light.directionZ = 1;

scene.setDirectionalLight(light);
```

Light3D

Light3D is the base class for 3-D lights. Instances of the Light3D class are not directly created by the developer.

Extends

```
EventTarget-Light3D
```

Common Properties

color: The color of the light source.

Common Methods

There are no common methods for Light3D other than the ones inherited from EventTarget.

Scene3D

The Scene3D class is the 3-D equivalent of the Scene class.

Inheritance

EventTarget-Scene3D

Common Properties

- backgroundColor: The background color of the Scene3D.
- childNodes: An array of child elements of the Scene3D.
- lights: An array of Light3D elements in the Scene3D.

Common Methods

All examples assume a variable, scene, has been created as an instance of the Scene3D class.

Method	Explanation	Example
addChild(sprite);	Adds a Sprite3D to the Scene3D.	scene.addChild(droid);
addLight(light);	Adds a light to the Scene3D.	scene.addLight(light3);
getAmbientLight();	Retrieves the ambient light source in the Scene3D.	scene.getAmbientLight();
getCamera();	Retrieves the camera source in the Scene3D.	scene.getCamera();
getDirectionalLight();	Retrieves the directional light source in the Scene3D.	scene.getDirectionalLight();
removeChild(sprite);	Deletes a Sprite3D from a Scene3D.	scene.removeChild(droid);
removeLight(light);	Deletes a Light3D from the Scene3D.	scene.removeLight(light2);
setAmbientLight(light);	Sets an ambient light source in the Scene3D.	scene.setAmbientLight(light2);
setCamera(camera);	Sets the active Camera3D inside of the Scene3D.	scene.setCamera(camera);
setDirectionalLight(light);	Sets the directional light source in the Scene3D.	scene.setDirectionalLigh(light6);

Example Use

```
var scene = new Scene3D();
var sprite = new Sprite3D();

scene.addChild(sprite);
```

Sprite3D

The Sprite3D class is the 3-D equivalent of the Sprite class.

Extends

EventTarget-Sprite3D

Common Properties

- childNodes: An array for child Sprite3D elements.

- scaleX: Scaling factor on the X axis.

- scaleY: Scaling factor on the Y axis.

- scaleZ: Scaling factor on the Z axis.

- x: Position of the Sprite3D on the X axis.

- y: Position of the Sprite3D on the Y axis.

- z: Position of the Sprite3D on the Z axis.

Common Methods

All examples assume a variable, droid, has been created as an instance of the Sprite3D class.

Method	Explanation	Example
addChild(sprite);	Adds a child Sprite3D to the Sprite3D object.	droid.addChild(droid2);
altitude(amount);	Moves a Sprite3D along the Y axis.	droid.altitude(2);
clone();	Duplicates the Sprite3D object.	droid.clone();
forward(amount);	Moves the Sprite3D along the Z axis.	droid.forward(2);
intersect(object);	Returns true if the Sprite3D is intersecting with the designated 3D object.	droid.intersect(droid2);
removeChild(sprite);	Removes a child Sprite3D object from the Sprite3D.	droid.removeChild(droid2);
rotatePitch(amount);	Rotates the Sprite3D along the X axis.	droid.rotatePitch(15);
rotateRoll(amount);	Rotates the Sprite3D along the Z axis.	droid.rotateRoll(15);
rotateYaw(amount);	Rotates the Sprite3D along the Y axis.	droid.rotateYaw(15);

(continued)

Method	Explanation	Example
scale(x,y,z);	Scales the Sprite3D along the x, y, and z axes.	droid.scale(2,2,2);
set(colladaFile);	Sets a Collada file as the model to be used for the Sprite3D.	droid.set(game.assets["images/droid.dae"]);
sidestep(amount);	Moves the Sprite3D along the X axis.	droid.sidestep(2);

ui.enchant.js

This plugin contains various elements to create a user interface for enchant.js games and supports various buttons, pads, and labels. For most classes, the required image must also be loaded into a given enchant.js game. Required images have the same name as their respective classes.

APad

This class is for an analog pad that can control movement in any two-dimensional direction.

Extends

EventTarget-Node-Group-APad

Common Properties

- isTouched: Returns true if the APad is currently being touched.

Common Methods

There are no common methods for APad other than the ones inherited from EventTarget, Node, and Group.

Button

This class creates a button with text on it that can be clicked by the player.

Extends

EventTarget-Node-Entity-Button

Common Properties

- color: The color of the text.
- font: The font of the text.
- size: The font size of the text.
- text: The text to be displayed on the button.

Common Methods

There are no common methods for `Button` other than the ones inherited from `EventTarget`, `Node`, and `Entity`.

Example Use

```
//Creates a virtual 'a' button at (260, 250) and adds it to the rootScene
abtn = new Button(260, 250, 'a');
```

LifeLabel

This class creates a label showing a number of hearts to represent a character's health.

Extends

This class is defined in the highest level of ui.enchant.js. It has no parent classes.

Common Properties

- `life`: The current life displayed by the `LifeLabel`.
- `maxLife`: The maximum amount of life displayed by the `LifeLabel`.
- `x`: The X position of the `LifeLabel`.
- `y`: The Y position of the `LifeLabel`.

Common Methods

This class has no methods.

MutableText

This class allows text to be displayed using an image for each of the characters, allowing the text to show up exactly the same across different operating systems and browsers.

Extends

This class is defined in the highest level of ui.enchant.js. It has no parent classes.

Common Properties

- `posX`: X position of the `MutableText` object.
- `posY`: Y position of the `MutableText` object.
- `text`: Text shown by the `MutableText` object.
- `width`: Width of the `MutableText` object in pixels.

Common Methods

All examples assume a variable, `message`, has been created as an instance of the `MutableText` class.

Method	Explanation	Example
`setText(text);`	Sets the text of the `MutableText` object.	`message.setText("Hello!");`

Pad

This class creates a four-direction directional pad for the player to interact with. When buttons on the pad are pressed, they issue `Events` corresponding to their direction (e.g., `UP`, `DOWN`, `LEFT`, `RIGHT`).

Extends

`EventTarget-Node-Entity-Sprite-Pad`

Common Properties

There are no common properties for `Pad` other than the ones inherited from `EventTarget`, `Node`, `Entity`, and `Sprite`.

Common Methods

There are no common methods for `Pad` other than the ones inherited from `EventTarget`, `Node`, `Entity`, and `Sprite`.

ScoreLabel

This class is a specially engineered version of the `MutableText` class designed to show the score of a game.

Extends

This class is defined in the highest level of ui.enchant.js. It has no parent classes.

Common Properties

- `score`: Specifies the score to be displayed by `ScoreLabel`.
- `x`: The X position of the `ScoreLabel`.
- `y`: The Y position of the `ScoreLabel`.

Common Methods

This class has no methods.

Index

CPSIA information can be obtained at www.ICGtesting.com
Printed in the USA
LVOW11s1456011013

354946LV00008B/486/P